THE SUCCESSF

*how 163 of the world's greatest en
adversity into success*

BY MATTHEW TURNER

FEATURING AJ LEON

Published by Turndog Publishing

Discover More At SuccessfulMistake.com

THE SUCCESSFUL MISTAKE CONTENTS

Although I'm the writer of this book, it took an army of incredible people to transform these pages from an idea into reality. I have so many people to thank, and I suppose I should begin with those 163 inspiring individuals who shared their own #greatmistake, so the rest of us can learn from their hardship.

You didn't have to jump on a call with me and offer your invaluable time, but you did. For this, I'm thankful beyond belief, and I'm so proud to have you part of this book. I only hope I did your stories justice.

I'd also like to thank a few amazing partners, whose support have helped me bring this book to life. These include Zvi and the team at Contactually, David and co. at Typeform, the wonderful guys and gals at FollowUp.cc, and the awesome folk at Scrivener.

I thank you all for your support, and I cannot wait to work a little magic with you in the future.

Then there are a few beautiful businesses I know, who decided to support this book before everyone else. I offered them the chance to grab an early bird book bundle, and they took me up on this offer because they desired to share it with their staff and customers.

As such, I'd like to thank James and the Blackhall Engineering team; Greg and Charlie at Splitpixel Design; Peter Bailey of Fail Forward; Helen Ots who leads Social Storm; Andrew Hopkins and the superstars at Moss Metal Finishing; Oliver North and the Rosenbauer Group; Peter Jones and the guys at Dynamic Management; and my main man, Arnold du Toit, and those who part of the Drive Daddy revolution.

You're a special bunch, and I'm lucky and grateful to have your epic support.

There are more to thank, of course, such as Bridget and Barnaby, who edited and perfected these very words. Without the both of you, this book would have remained incomplete, and I'm proud to have you part of this journey.

And then there are those amazing readers who open my emails, reply to them, speak to me online, and have helped guide me whilst I wrote this book. There are too many of you to mention by name, but I imagine you know who you are. You've been here from the beginning, and I cannot put into words what your support means to me. Thank you.

Finally, I wouldn't be here without those I know; my friends, my family, my peers.

This adventure I'm on is full of ups and downs, and you guys are my constant. You're there for me when I need it, and put up with me far too often. Again, there are too many of you to mention by name, but I sure hope you know who you are.

Finally finally, I'd like to thank my parents for supporting me like no others; Rosanna for being the love of my life and helping me see a different kind of light; and to my best bud and partner in crime, George (A.K.A. The Kid, A.K.A. Kid Turndog), because without you I'd have nothing to write about, period.

Thank you, thank you, and thank you some more. I love you all.

With this, I'd like to welcome you to *The Successful Mistake*, and to save my final thanks to you, the reader, because you've chosen to read this book, and this means an awful lot. Cheers, and here's to the adventure ahead of us.

Dedicated to my muse, The Kid. You are my success and everything that accompanies it.

HAVE YOU DOWNLOADED YOUR FREE INTERACTIVE WORKBOOKS?

The Successful Mistake is designed to Entertain, Inspire & Educate you, and in a bid to take your reading experience to the next level, each stage within this book ends with a Tasks & Takeaways section. This allows you to implement what you learn straight away, and to make your life easier, you can download a series of free interactive workbooks by visiting:

successfulmistake.com/takeaways

A FOREWORD BY AJ LEON

I first met Matthew when he hosted a book tour event to promote an essay collection that I had published. The event took place in Sowerby Bridge, a market town in Matthew's beautiful home county of Yorkshire – unfamiliar territory for a Cuban who cut his teeth in New York. I knew we'd be firm friends when he handed me one of his famous homemade toasties at 1am after we'd shared a few pints in his local pub to thank him for hosting such a wonderful event.

With his first publication of this kind, Matthew has taken on one of the hardest but also the most important topics. Learning from failures is a wonderful skill. The trick is to have them be the springboard for future successes. But it's hardwon. My own journey certainly hasn't been easy; very few worth taking are. Failure can spawn the seeds of success, but it can be difficult to pick them out amongst the ashes. Matthew is a natural storyteller with a great talent for narrative and imagery, and The Successful Mistake shares its lessons and advice in powerful, beguiling language. At the same time, there is no fluff here: his takeaways are coldpressed advice, gleaned the hard way, and laid out in terms which makes them immediately actionable.

As The Successful Mistake explores, everybody fails. The difference is that some people allow this initial failure to entirely define them. They permit this one misstep to become the day that they bend a knee and acquiesce to a fear that will hold to ransom the dreams they once dreamed, which will forever rot in the chambers of their hearts, and the unwritten pages of their Moleskins.

Others, however, convert this failure into something much better, and set about creating a phoenix from the ashes, simply by changing their approach, analysing what went wrong, and learning from their earlier stumbles. Matthew's book is testament to the incredible potential inherent in any mistake. There are

163 top business minds in here that discovered the same thing that I did: namely that a mistake can be the best thing that's ever happened to you. But this discovery is a tricky one; one that's hard to acknowledge, hard to work with and hard to convert back into success.

The book you are holding in your hands holds the clues of how to begin this process of entrepreneurial alchemy. Matthew's interviews are incisive and illuminating. The wisdom they contain will enable you to learn more from your mistakes than you do from even your successes. With The Successful Mistake, Matthew aimed to ,entertain, educate, and inspire' – he has done all this and more. Perhaps the highest praise I can give is that I sincerely wish I'd had the book in my hands when in 2008 I tossed out a life that wasn't working for me, and began the long slow work of converting my life's failure into a success. Overcoming adversity isn't easy, but it's easier with guidebooks like this one. You are in for a great read.

AN INTRODUCTION

For a few seconds I was fine. Then panic kicked into gear and consumed me, sending shivers over my skin and a nauseous thud throughout my stomach. 'What have I done?' I whispered. 'I've made a mistake. I can't do this.'

I was *terrified*.

Some people grow up with the dream of owning their own company and taking charge of an empire. Not me. For the longest of times, I aspired to climb the corporate ladder and become a vital cog in a grander machine. When you work for other people, there's less stress and more security. Working for myself... Nope, that wasn't for me.

So why did I lie paralysed in bed, pinned under the covers, realising I'd become a self-employed man? Why had I welcomed unemployment with open arms in the belief I'd find greater happiness by taking charge of my own destiny?

I remember this shitty morning like it was yesterday, my alarm barking to life at an unruly hour because I wanted to get up and start my new existence with a bang. Like I say, for a few brief seconds all was fine, but the peace didn't last.

'What have I done?' I whispered again, clinging to my cover like a little boy, afraid of the dark.

As you read these words, I'm positive you'll relate to such worry, fear, and self-doubt. Maybe you've already had a morning like this, or maybe your entrepreneurial journey has yet to begin. Either way, you nod your head and agree; I write this with confidence, because I've interviewed 163 successful entrepreneurs for this book.

These are people with money, fame, and freedom, yet they still have stories of worry, fear and self-doubt to share. It doesn't matter how esteemed or wealthy an individual is, they still suffer the same worries that I did that morning, and they continue to make mistakes and fail to this day.

The only difference is that they approach such scenarios differently from the way that I did (although it took me the process of writing this book before I was able to figure out how they do).

It's now your turn to unearth such life-changing lessons, but before you do, I'd like to focus a little more on this horrendous first day because that's where this book began. You see, as I lay in bed unable to move, I considered the previous few months of employment and security.

I wouldn't say I loved my job, but I didn't hate it, either. The money was good. The potential, exciting. Life, overall... Pretty darn spiffy.

But it was around this time that I began to blog and delve into the online world. I wrote more, discovered new people, and befriended folk who lived a life on their own terms. All of a sudden, the corporate ladder climb didn't seem so sweet, nor did my daily nine-to-five grind. I yearned for more, and what had started as a mere rumble exploded into life when my boss, Tony, called me into his office.

'I want to change your role in the company, ' he said. 'You're doing well, but going forward I'd like you to focus on...'

It was no use. His words evaporated into nothing as I drifted off into my own thoughts. I was different from the rest of the team, always keen to experiment and implement *new* processes, which in the beginning was great, but I soon sensed this rubbed certain folk the wrong way. As I look back on my twenties, I now see that I was a terrible employee at each and every job, and it was during this short meeting with Tony that I realised just how bad I was.

I also realised I faced three choices:

✓   Take the new role and grow frustrated.

✓   Get a new job and more than likely grow frustrated.

✓   Work for myself and build a life on my own terms, like those I admired online.

I'm sure you can guess the choice I made, which led to this morning of paralysis a few weeks later. I hopped into bed the night before, a free man in waiting, complete with a long to-do list and mind hefty with dreams. I drifted off into sleep with a plan, knowing how I'd spend my first day of entrepreneurship. A few hours later, I woke up and clung to my sheets like a child. Holding back the tears, I stared at my to-do list, terrified to tackle a single task, because I didn't know which one deserved the most attention.

I feared failure, so chose to do nothing at all.

Each passing second drained me of confidence and belief, and I even considered calling Tony and pleading for my job back. I felt worthless and useless, and, as I slipped deeper into my self-pity, I did the one thing I could bring myself to do: email those who had been through this before, who owned their own businesses, who lived the life I apparently wished to live. After all, I'd just spent months befriending a bunch of entrepreneurs and online go-getters. These people were now my peers and had advice to offer, and although I only completed one task that day, luckily for me it turned out to be the most important one of all.

WE LEARN MORE FROM OUR STRUGGLES THAN OUR SUCCESSES

Over the next few days I Skyped, coffeed, and conversed with numerous entrepreneurs and business owners. As they shared stories and advice, a particular theme wove its way through each conversation, because for some reason these people chose to focus on their mistakes and failures.

I couldn't believe it. I'd figured they'd offer success stories and build up my confidence, not torture me with their hardships.

'Do you know something,' I said to my buddy, Arnold, tapping my chin. 'You're the fifth person I've spoken to these last few days, and each one of you has focused on your mistakes. Why are you telling me all this?' I whined. 'I already feel close to giving up.'

Gazing above his webcam, Arnold smiled. 'I guess we learn more from our mistakes than our successes.'

Lifting me from my self-induced fog, clarity reigned supreme as these numerous conversations intermingled into a single cohesive epiphany.

You see, people like you and me start new businesses each day.

We're scared and cautious and overthink everything, and although you have your dreams and goals, and believe in what you're doing, it's easy to slip into a glass-half-empty mentality. You fear making mistakes. You fear failure. You compare yourself to those you admire, which makes it impossible for you to succeed. You're so worried about committing to one idea, you choose to play it safe and do nothing at all. Or worse, you become bogged down with lots of little ideas and become a master of none. It's understandable, because we're brought up to fear and avoid failure and mistakes.

It's red ink on your homework; it's failed exams and tests; it's rejection; it's a job you don't like but have to take; it's pressure from your parents and teachers; it's the media and stardom and bright lights of Hollywood; it's the fact that if you don't have a particular degree, or drive a certain type of car, you're deemed not quite good enough.

Is it any wonder you fear mistakes and failure? Is it any wonder you begin a new venture with such hope, but soon drown under self-doubt and insecurity? The truth is we're born to make mistakes and fail again and again.

I recall my beautiful son learning to walk, and the tears and frustration and bumps and bruises. It didn't come easily, but each tumble took him closer to those all-important first steps. He garbled a lot before he learned to speak. Sometimes you have to burn yourself in order to appreciate it isn't a good idea to touch fire.

During this conversation with Arnold, I saw these worries and fears in a new light. I realised that those I spoke with weren't warning me, or kicking me further down, rather they were helping me to see that this entrepreneurial journey isn't perfect, and isn't without hardship, and although it may be hard to believe, we don't become successful despite our failures, but because of them.

A NEW MINDSET FOR A NEW AGE

A few weeks later, I walked through London whilst visiting Arnold.

'After talking to you, I knew what I had to do,' I said to him. 'I like to think that I value mistakes and the lessons that come from them, but I've not been doing this of late. I've allowed them to hold me back, and the truth is it's because I'm scared. I don't know what lies ahead of me, and it's terrifying, man. But I guess most people feel like this when they begin a business. Hell, maybe you always do in part. So, I've got this idea for a book, and...'

I continued to tell Arnold all about this idea, which, many moons later, rests in your hands as you read these words. I didn't plan to write this book when I first left my job, but it was that dreaded first day that inspired me to do so.

You live in a world of opportunity but absolute chaos. The Internet has not only brought us closer together, it's pushed us further apart. There's so much *stuff* and white noise, and so long as there is, your self-doubt and insecurity will continue to creep into your life.

And just like it stifled me, it may stifle you, too. It stops you from fulfilling your version of success because you continue to worry about not reaching the lofty heights of your idols.

And know this, my friend; you cannot stop yourself from making mistakes. You can, however, learn to deal with them and transform these situations into life-changing ones. This is what the world's most successful people do, and after interviewing 163 of them, I'm excited to share what sets them apart.

If you're the type of person who believes you have it figured out, and live a life of perfection already, this book isn't for you. If you're happy to plod along and remain safe and content, this book is not for you. But if you desire success and to build a life on your own terms, this is a book you need.

These pages aren't jammed with one case study after another, simply throwing more useless content at your face. The journey you're about to begin guides you through a seven stage process of intention and purpose. It's designed to show you how the world's most successful people deal with adversity, and how you can too. It's written to not only inspire you, but to give you the necessary tools to build your own version of a successful mistake. I interviewed 163 successful go-getters, spent 100+ hours on Skype, sent over 1,000 emails, and dedicated over three years of my life to this book so that you can learn how the world's greatest minds approach their failures and transform them into success.

If this doesn't sound like something you wish to be part of, close the book and go and read another one. If it does, I invite you to turn the page and unravel what this unique seven-stage-process has in store for you, because it may just change how you approach your business and your life from here on in.

THE SEVEN STAGES OF YOUR #GREATMISTAKE

If you glance over the contents page, you may notice there are seven stages within this book that resemble the seven stages of grief. Well, there's a reason for this; I've structured the book around the process so often linked to losing a loved one.

The thing is, this process doesn't only cover what you go through during grief, but rather change in general.

We're creatures of habit, you see, and when thrust out of your comfort zone it sends you into a maze of emotion. So, when you make a mistake or fail (or simply begin a new venture or idea), you invite change into your life. You're no longer comfortable in your habit, so you find yourself going through a particular type of process:

1) Shock

2) Pain

3) Bargaining

4) Depression

5) Tipping Point

6) Reconstruction

7) Acceptance

Sometimes it's a subtle journey; on other occasions it redefines your entire world. Each mistake, failure, and scenario differs, but no matter what your situation is, you go through this process each time. It may not always be as clear-cut or as simple as moving from one step to the other, but undoubtedly these are the stages you go through.

This isn't a psychology book though, so when it comes to knowledge of the brain and how and why you do what you do, you should not, under any circumstance, listen to me.

I'm a rather simple man, with a simple brain, but I've gone through these stages myself (as I'm sure you have).

As a writer, I have a tendency to make up words and mingle theories together, so although these seven stages should act as an inspiration, don't for a second expect a theoretical textbook. That's not how I do things, and I do not apologise for this.

What you can expect are several chapters within each stage, all of which represent a different topic and set of takeaways. Within these you'll meet successful entrepreneurs and their mistake-riddled stories, designed to bring the words you read to life in an entertaining manner.

There are tips and tricks and tasks throughout, as well as exclusive content you can devour online, because I don't want you to read this book once and then forget about it. This is a book you'll want to highlight, and place strips of paper between the pages, so you can come back to when you need it.

And trust me, as you delve deeper into your own entrepreneurial journey, you will need it.

Finally, I've approached each chapter and sub-chapter as an individual blog post, and although I encourage you to work through this book step-by-step, you can, if you wish, mix things up and pick and choose which chapter to read.

But, before I let you venture forward and weave your way through these pages, there's something you must know, and someone you must meet. He goes by the name of Mark, and he has something rather important to tell you.

THE UNFASHIONABLE FASHION OF MISTAKES

Before you delve into Stage One: Shock, I'd like to introduce you to Mark Schaefer; a wonderful and successful entrepreneur who turned our interview upside down with a rather different viewpoint on mistakes.

'You know, it's really fashionable right now to talk about big mistakes. Somehow it's become cool for entrepreneurs to make them, like it's a badge of courage or something. But here's the secret to business success: Don't make big mistakes,' he said.

Although I've encountered every imaginable viewpoint along this journey, Mark's words stuck with me. I value mistakes and believe they can form the catalyst for your greatest idea yet, but I don't wish to glorify them. You shouldn't either, nor should you set out to make them.

This book's purpose isn't to glorify your mistakes, or failures; rather to help you appreciate the value they offer, so long as you approach them with the right mindset. It's written to help you look past the pain and find the potential growth beyond it. It's designed to introduce you to those who have been there and done it before, appreciate how they overcome their mistakes and learn from them, and better yourself by living through their eyes.

My role as the writer of this book is to help you:

✓ Discover what success means to you, and dedicate your life towards this.

✓ Overcome your fear of failure, so it doesn't stop you from achieving greatness.

✓ Learn how to spot your mistakes before they happen, and transform them into success when they do.

✓ Work through the seven stages of your great mistake with a successful and confident mindset.

✓   Stand shoulder to shoulder with those you admire, instead of spending your life looking up to them.

Mark's right. We shouldn't make mistakes and failure desirable, because the whole point of business (and indeed, living a happy and free life) is to avoid such hardship. I don't wake up each day hoping I fail. I don't invite mistakes into my life. But I do appreciate that they happen and don't let them define me when they do.

As Mark says himself, 'It's okay to make little ones. In fact, you can't help but make little ones. Just avoid the big ones because these are what kill your business. Nobody sets out to be a failure. Why glorify it?'

So, let's listen to Mark and not glorify our mistakes, failure, or pain. Instead, let's understand them, learn how to spot them, appreciate what it takes to overcome them, and better ourselves like the world's most successful people do.

This begins with Stage One: Shock; a stage that not only focuses on the key attributes of a mistake and how they form in the first place, but also the preceding warning signs, that are so often present in our everyday lives.

Spotting these signs is another matter altogether, but in the coming pages, you'll start to appreciate how to, and indeed learn to control yourself when that moment of shock arrives.

HAVE YOU DOWNLOADED YOUR FREE INTERACTIVE WORKBOOKS?

The Successful Mistake is designed to Entertain, Inspire & Educate you, and in a bid to take your reading experience to the next level, each stage within this book ends with a Tasks & Takeaways section. This allows you to implement what you learn straight away, and to make your life easier, you can download a series of free interactive workbooks by visiting:

successfulmistake.com/takeaways

INTRODUCING OUR CHAPTER PARTNER,
TYPEFORM

op·por·tu·ni·ty cost

noun ECONOMICS

noun: **opportunity cost**; plural noun: **opportunity costs**

1. the loss of potential gain from other alternatives when one alternative is chosen.

Here's the dilemma: Do you maximise returns in the short run, keep your promises, but go against your values; or do you not keep your promises, and sacrifice those short-term gains for a potentially better result?

Sometimes you know a business decision will hurt profits and it's so obvious to everyone that it doesn't make sense to go against the data. But that's exactly what we did. We went against the data and sacrificed money and profitability. Although we couldn't quantify the true cost of our decision, we understood its impact.

My name is Paul Campillo, and I work at Typeform, located in sunny Barcelona. Typeform allows you to build web forms, surveys, quizzes, and simple apps into a slick conversational interface. It's this 'slick conversational interface' that makes our product remarkable. And that word 'remarkable' caused a whole lot of trouble and led to that costly decision.

Let me explain.

THE REMARKABLE MISTAKE

In July of 2015, a small group of staff got together to work on our brand guidelines and communication standards. This included long meetings about company vision, mission and values. We also dug into typography, brand colours, and what values would decide all future products and content.

And somewhere in that process, the word 'remarkable' sprung up. It was persistent and finally stuck. Put simply, everything we produce at Typeform, whether it's a product or a piece of content must adhere to these four values: *it must be simple, friendly, useful, and remarkable.*

No small feat, but something we all agreed would guide future decisions when it comes to making things. If there's a debate about whether something should launch, well, our product values would be the tie-breaker.

Is this simple, friendly, useful, and remarkable?

No? Then hold the fort.

Yes? Then launch away.

It wouldn't be long before those values were put to the test. In October, days before we launched our new blog to the public, David Okuniev, co-founder of Typeform, stared intently at his screen. He studied the revamped blog design for a few more seconds and without even looking my way said, 'We can't launch like this.'

Oh man. We told the public we'd launch our blog in September so we were already a month late. Of course I knew why. The blog wasn't right. The design, the layout, the typography, the feel. The line spacing was off. We couldn't distinguish paragraphs from each other. But even more than that, the blog wasn't remarkable. It looked like something that already existed. And we all knew it.

In a conversation with Sançar, our head of content, we asked, 'What if we delayed the launch a little longer to get the design right? To do something truly remarkable?'

Sançar set up a meeting to discuss this decision. There was a lot of back and forth, but the one thing that kept coming up was the opportunity cost. What's the opportunity cost of not launching the blog? Every day we don't blog and put content out into the world, we miss out on new users. We miss out on brand awareness.

VALUE OR MONEY

Let's see. A potential 300% monthly traffic spike was left on the table. That's a lot of new users, which translates to a lot of moolah. As author Seth Godin once observed, 'Content marketing is all the marketing that's left.'

And every day that we weren't out there helping people make educated purchase decisions, or helping people get the most out of their research efforts, or helping current users get the most out of their Typeform experience, they were getting it from someone else.

Let's face it. Not having a blog in 2015 is like not having a website in 2005. We're invisible.

But that word 'remarkable' snuck into our rational brains. Would we make our decision based on money or values? Pedro, our director of marketing, reminded us of the opportunity cost. The loss in revenue. The loss in retention. The loss in acquisition.

We gathered in a small circle, and voted on the final outcome — it wasn't unanimous but we decided to delay the blog launch until January 2016 and redesign it from the ground up. There was disappointment and added pressure.

But you know that things rarely go according to plan, right? Well, this was no exception. Three months turned into six and the blog finally went live during the final week of March 2016.

Was delaying the blog a mistake? Sure. It cost us. We miscalculated resources and timelines that extended the delay an additional three months. We lost six months of traffic and potential new users. We lost six months of positioning ourselves as a content leader in our space.

But now we have a remarkable blog. Our SaaS peers have expressed 'blog envy'. Our team is proud of what we produced. And our co-founders, Robert and David, can share this lesson of sticking to your values, and not succumbing to the pressure of short-term profits.

The word 'sacrifice' essentially means to give up something of value for something of greater value. We all knew what we'd be sacrificing with our decision to delay, but in the end the greater value is what matters. And for the good people at Typeform, the greater value was clear: *be remarkable.*

And that's why Matthew wrote this book. He's here to remind you that 'remarkable' is on the other side of those mistakes. Although all mistakes can't be 'taken back', they contain lessons that make you better at what you do. But you must persist. You must move forward. Stick to your values. Sure, learn, make changes, correct course, but embrace your mistakes because they inevitably lead to one place: success.

Matthew has interviewed over 160 successful people in the world of entrepreneurship, authors, bloggers, coaches, and consultants. The pot of gold he's uncovered for you in the form of anecdotes and stories are invaluable, and this all begins with Stage One: Shock.

STAGE 1: **THAT AWKWARD MOMENT WHEN THE SHIT HITS THE FAN**

After blogging for six months, and seeing little in return, Jaime Masters came close to giving up. As she prepared her farewell email to her subscribers, something stopped her; a nagging something. Such procrastinating often ends badly, but on this occasion it turned out for the best.

CNN called wanting to interview her about how she cleared $70,000 of debt and began a life of blogging. You may assume that this is a good thing, although it marked the beginning of Jaime's greatest mistake.

'I prepared my site for an up-spike in traffic for my CNN feature, but not for my face to appear on Yahoo's homepage,' she said, recalling a time before she interviewed hundreds of millionaires for her podcast, *The Eventual Millionaire*. 'My site crashed, and remained down for days. When it came back online, I realised how much potential traffic and how many opportunities I'd lost.'

I'm sure you'd love to go viral yourself, but are you prepared for this? Because amid Jaime's ecstasy and excitement of going viral, the shock and realisation soon hit. But this isn't the part of

Jamie's story that's the most important, because a few months later the unthinkable happened.

'I assumed it was a fluke, that I wouldn't get that sort of exposure again.' Shaking her head, she laughed. 'Not long after, I appeared on Yahoo's homepage again, and again, my site crashed.'

The shock of the unexpected is one thing, but the shock of reliving the same pain twice... now that's a different kind of agony.

'Oh, it hurt,' she said. 'Stupid too, because I could have changed my hosting rather easily. I managed to gather some metrics this time, and in the two hours my site stayed up, I received over 8,000 visitors.' She shook her head again. 'I remained on Yahoo's homepage for a further forty-eight hours, and all the while my site stayed down. I kept thinking about those lost visitors, but couldn't handle it. Like I say, it hurt.'

It's amazing how a great opportunity can turn sour rather quickly, but that's the thing about shock; it shocks you.

In Stage One: Shock, we focus on those dreaded moments that slow you to a standstill. They begin in your stomach, rumble up your chest, and then continue through your brain and out of your mouth as an 'Oh no! What have I done?'

Jaime experienced this moment of shock at a time when she should have been celebrating and jumping for joy; exposure on Yahoo's homepage is the zenith for all aspiring bloggers, after all.

I've watched successful entrepreneurs relive such awful moments many times throughout this journey, and however big or small their mistake may be, those initial moments of stress, pain, and shock are enough to unnerve even the hardest-nosed entrepreneur.

This is what we'll focus on over the coming pages: unearthing the attributes of a mistake and the various forms they take. You'll explore the warning signs, and see that even when this shock comes as a surprise, the telltale clues are there all along. We'll then finish with some actionable tasks and takeaways because although you cannot always escape your mistakes, you can prepare for them.

You may deem it unfortunate to begin this book by focusing on such tough periods, but in fact this is where your journey begins. Before you can overcome your mistakes and failures, you must first understand what they look like, what they're made of, and how they came to be. From here, you can spot them before they happen, and overcome them when they do. As you read Stage One: Shock — and indeed, the rest of this book — remember that you'll soon know how to tackle it in the same way as those you admire.

With this in mind, let's delve into some stories that are sure to make you cringe, grit your teeth, and sigh in disbelief...

THE ART OF HIRING PEOPLE

As an entrepreneur, you have to hire people. Some businesses require more staff than others, and maybe all you need is a team of virtual assistants or freelancers. It doesn't matter; a hire's a hire, my fellow hustler, and the odds are that you'll make a few bad ones.

To an extent, it's unavoidable and part of building a thriving culture. After all, people let you down. They don't achieve what you hope they will. They talk a good game, but produce a terrible one, and you must break through the rock before you unearth the diamonds.

Yet, it's the mistake that so many successful entrepreneurs look back on and wish they'd approached differently — *not because of the actual hire, but because of their poor judgement —* they've hired 'just anyone' instead of finding the right someone.

Or, as Rameet Chawla suggests, 'You should hire those you want, not those you need.'

The truth is that most bad hires aren't down to the person doing the woeful job, but rather the guy or gal who hired them in the first place. Hiring mistakes come down to poor judgement; your poor judgement, and it not only leaves you hurting (because let's face it, firing anyone — especially a friend — hurts), but it damages your business as a whole.

There are real costs to a failed hire, as well as invisible ones. And although you can't guarantee everyone you hire will become an absolute superstar, you can ensure you don't build a team around poor and desperate judgement.

There's an art to hiring, and it has little to do with the actual hire, it's more about making sure you don't fire them a week, a month, or a year, down the line. It's a tricky beast to master, and a mistake that often falls under one of three topics: hiring friends, hiring the cheap option, or hiring the rockstar.

BEWARE WHEN HIRING YOUR FRIENDS:

Before I sat down to chat with Jordan Harbinger, I knew him as a guy with lots of crazy stories; including kidnappings and other life-threatening tales. His hiring mistake may not have costs lives, but when it comes to moments of incredulous shock, it doesn't get much better, or should I say worse, than this.

'I remember having a conversation with my business partner once,' he said, describing his moment of misguided madness. 'We tried to create a new position for this one guy because he wasn't good at any role we slotted him into.'

Considering that Jordan's empire, *The Art of Charm*, began life as a humble podcast, it's understandable it grew organically. After reaching a certain level of success, he and his partners had to hire people, and so he did what most new entrepreneurs do; he approached friends, friends of friends, and those he knew.

Now, hiring friends isn't a problem per se, because we all have talented buddies, but if you hire them because it's quick and relatively painless, you have to ask yourself if it is the right hire, or the easy one.

If it's the latter, you may find yourself in Jordan's shoes, creating new roles in a bid to avoid firing your best pal.

'I remember showering later that day,' he continued, his tone a mixture of embarrassment and amusement. 'I thought to myself, "Did I really spend thirty minutes figuring out a new role for someone, in order to justify paying him a lot of money?"'

Whether you're new to business or not, it's clear this is a rather counter-intuitive approach that's sure to hurt your empire. You hire people to do a job, and to take issues off your plate, not produce more stress. But here was Jordan, spending his valuable time looking for ways to avoid firing a friend, and worse, paying him a handsome sum for the displeasure.

Now, you may be thinking to yourself, 'what an idiot'. And, to an extent, Jordan agrees with you, but be honest with yourself and imagine what you would do in the same situation. As an entrepreneur, you have a million tasks on your agenda, and this number rarely decreases. It's understandable that you would take the path of least resistance, especially when it comes to dealing with a friend or someone you know.

Hiring the right person is hard, whereas hiring anyone is easy.

To reiterate, the art of hiring doesn't lie in the hire, but instead in ensuring that you don't have to fire. That isn't to say that working with friends can't work; I've met lots of entrepreneurs who do and see their business thrive because of it. But this only happens if they're the right person for the job. If they aren't, and instead you hire them because it's the easy or cheap option, you set yourself up for a lot of hardship further down the line.

As Jordan said to me, 'If there's one thing worse than hiring friends, it's firing them.'

During this first stage of your #greatmistake, you suffer shock. Whether this lasts for minutes, or weeks, your shock leads to pain and hurt, and the moment you involve something personal, like firing a friend or loved one… well, you tell me how you'd react. This all stems from poor judgment because you make the choice to hire anyone rather than the right someone.

You have jobs to do, and limited money, so you turn to your friends for help. Understandable, right? Something I'd argue every single entrepreneur has done at some point in time, which is why it's hard to judge Jordan too harshly. But that moment of shock when you stand in the shower and realise you're literally throwing money down the drain… well, you begin to question your judgment and ask why you hired said person in the first place.

Again, is it because it's the right hire to make or because it was the easiest? In Jordan's case it was the latter, but this big mistake redefined how he grew *The Art of Charm* and transformed its thriving culture into what it is today.

When it comes to hiring friends, each decision you make is laden with danger.

You're tempted into taking the easy path, instead of the right one, which is why it's a mistake so many successful entrepreneurs wish they could take back — yet at the same time they understand that it has taught them how valuable their team and culture is in the first place.

But what if you don't hire your friends? What if you have investment and money, and can build an experienced team full of expertise and skill?

You may think it's a shortcut to success, with little risk, but as you're about to find out, this isn't always the case.

THE DANGER OF HIRING AN ALL STAR TEAM

When you own a business that goes head to head with the likes of Etsy, it's important to stand out and leave a lasting impression, which is why Jon Crawford — the founder of StorEnvy — focussed his initial hiring efforts around building a superstar team.

'I tried to design a company culture built on rockstars,' said Jon, from his contemporary San Francisco office. 'I intentionally found designers who had their own following and were people of "note", but quickly realised we weren't getting anything done. We weren't releasing anything. We weren't shipping anything. The reason for this was that we weren't on the same page, because when you're a rockstar it's hard to play a supporting role in someone else's band.'

Considering he'd just seed-funded his start-up, and had the money to go after the best, Jon took an understandable approach. He also existed in a thriving industry, where platforms like Etsy showed consumers a new model and approach. With huge potential, and the need to move fast, going after the headline-hitting designer seemed to make sense. Surely, building an all-star team would result in greater riches than a bunch of up and coming go-getters.

Well, it comes back to judgement and doing the right thing for you and your business. Where a bootstrapped start-up may lose focus, and go after the cheap and easy hire (approaching friends and the like), a heavily funded one might go wobbly at the knees over that superstar exec.

But poor judgment isn't prejudiced; poor judgment is poor judgment in any form it takes, and the moment you hire someone for the wrong reason becomes the moment you set yourself up to fire them further down the line. This, in turn, leads to hiring someone else... wasting more money... losing more time... straining your resources.

It was something Jon had to do a lot of because he reached an impasse where he knew he had to make changes.

'I had to let everyone go, and return to zero employees, because we weren't building the right culture; we weren't getting anything done,' he said. 'And it was tough because I had to call each investor one-by-one and tell them what I'd done; that we were back to having zero employees again.'

Not only this, but Jon also had to take each of these superstar employees out for coffee and tell them it was time to move on. That's no easy feat at all, as it not only wasted his time and resources (let alone the months that it set the company back), but it tested his resolve as a leader and founder.

'The strange thing is, I hired our first great employee a few days after all this happened, and we've continued to bring great people on board since. It's all about finding the right people now, and ensuring they fit into the culture we continue to build. You need to cultivate a culture like this over time, whereas I think I went into it desiring a cool company and believing all I'd have to do was hire cool people and the rest would follow. But you can't just create or buy 'cool'; you have to build it and nurture it with real people working towards a real vision.'

I'm sure you can empathise with Jon's decision to hire the best, because it makes sense to build an experienced team when you have the money and foundation to do so. But like he says, you cannot buy a thriving culture, merely craft one over time and with purpose. As such, how much, or how little, money you spend on your team becomes somewhat unimportant. It's about crafting the right one, and you do this by making the right decisions, the right hires; putting your best judgment forward at all times.

Jon's not alone in taking this path; in fact I've connected with many entrepreneurs who assumed the headline-hitting executive would result in good times for all.

Sometimes it does. Other times, not so much.

There's no magic formula for how much you should spend, which brings us to the final piece of the hiring puzzle, because going after the cheaper option has the power to unnerve your world, too.

Which is where our friend Rameet Chawla, who we met earlier, joins this tale…

WHEN THE CHEAP OPTION ISN'T CHEAP AT ALL:

As founder of Fueled, one of New York's hippest and fastest growing app agencies, Rameet has hired an array of talent in recent years. Listening to him roll one story off after another, one in particular stopped me in my tracks.

'I believe in hiring people who are better than me, and surrounding myself with people who are smarter, which I did for our core services like design and development, but in order to reduce overheads I hired cheaper resources (like interns) for our operations and back-office management.'

Once again, I'm sure you can relate to, and appreciate, Rameet's thought process, because there are certain roles within a business that aren't as vital. That's not to say they're unimportant, but they don't hold as much urgency. Which is true, in part, until you begin to unravel the numerous costs associated with a bad hire (or should we say wrong hire), and appreciate how expensive cheap can be.

'Something that hurt our initial growth was not hiring talented people,' Rameet continued. 'Most of the time you don't hire talent because you perceive it to be more expensive, so you end up bringing someone cheaper on board, right? Well, this is fine, but you usually end up hiring a second person too, and two junior members often cost the same as one experienced person. And the thing is, that one senior person is so much better than those two juniors combined.'

As one story led into another, Rameet considered another period, not long after this junior-hiring fiasco, and if that particular tale had stopped me in my tracks, this one knocked me off my feet completely.

'This one time, we hired a sales person,' he said, shaking his head. 'Over a three month period, we lost every lead assigned to them. If you consider the potential income lost, all because we hired a cheaper staff member, it's huge. We usually convert at 20-30%, and with a standard project creating $50,000 of revenue, the lost opportunity from this one poor hire hit us hard.'

These words changed how I saw hiring mistakes from then on.

It's one thing to consider the actual cost of a person's salary or car, but to think about the invisible costs, the potential money left on the table, and the revenue that could have been if only you hired the right someone... this changes everything.

A hiring mistake — be it friend related, going after the expensive option, or taking the cheap route — drags real and measurable costs along with it.

You can measure and put a value on things like salary, training, and advertising for a new role, but the moment you consider aspects like potential revenue left on the table, your time wasted as you shadow them or push them to be better, and the emotional strain that firing someone you care about brings; these are much harder to place a value on, and when it comes to shock they're almost always more shocking.

As an entrepreneur and business owner, you hire people to make your life easier, take tasks off your plate, and help your business grow. There's no other reason to bring someone on board, which is why so many successful entrepreneurs consider their greatest failure to be the way they approached hiring people, once upon a time. It isn't so much to do with the people they hired, rather the poor judgment they showed.

Firing a friend shocks you and leads to a great deal of pain;

often, long-lasting pain.

Realising that you wasted a lot of money on trying to buy a culture hurts, and has the power to halt your business before it gets going.

Finding out that your cheap hire wasn't cheap at all, and not only that, but realising the potential money and growth that's left on the table... All because you took the easy option, the quick option, the poor and wrong option..., It's shocking.

'Hire those you want, rather than those you need.'

The moment Rameet said this to me, I wrote it down and highlighted it; something I encourage you to do, too.

As an entrepreneur, it's easier to take the path of least resistance, not because you're lazy or stupid, but because you're busy and have a million tasks on your to-do list. But you hire people to relieve your burden, not add to it. You strive to build a thriving culture so you can grow and succeed, not to have it hold you back.

Whether your hiring mistake revolves around bringing a buddy on board, overpaying that all-star exec, or pinching the pennies and reaching out to anyone, it comes down to your poor judgment. So when that moment of shock hits, remember this. Remember it's down to you, not the person you hired. You brought the wrong person on board instead of searching for the right someone... The one person you want, not need.

But remember, it isn't the end of your journey; a bad hire won't end you. This is the beginning, and an opportunity to ensure you do build that thriving culture full of people who excel at what they do, make your life easier, and help your business grow.

Now let's not get ahead of ourselves, because before we get into that, we must first consider a few other key attributes. This brings us to a topic inextricably linked to hiring people: growth and expansion.

After all, I'm sure you have ambitions to grow, yes?

Well, you may like to rethink your plans after you read what comes next.

INSPIRED BY STORIES FROM: JORGAN HARBINGER, EMMA AGESE, ZEKE CAMUSIO, JON CRAWFORD, MIKE EILERTSEN, RAMEET CHAWLA, BEN KRUEGER, EMERSON SPARTZ, PAIGE ARNOF-FENN, ZOE JACKSON

THE DANGERS OF GROWTH & EXPANSION

You're an entrepreneur who strives to grow and expand your business, right?

It's a fundamental aspect of starting one in the first place, because you don't want to sit back and settle for the nine-to-five. There's nothing wrong with such a life, but it isn't for you. Why else would you read a book about entrepreneurs and go-getting thought leaders? Yet, despite its fundamental presence in your entrepreneurial world, the road to growth and expansion remains perilous with danger and worrying twists and turns.

You'd think that such a foundational aspect of business would have a more definitive solution, but I'm afraid it doesn't, and like mistakes in hiring, mistakes with growth and expansion are some of the most common mistakes I've come across during these interviews. Again and again you're going to face the proposition: to grow or not to grow…

You'd choose growth each and every time, right? It is, after all, what your whole entrepreneurial journey is about. Growth means touching shoulders with your idols. It results in money in the bank. Investors come to you, rather than you begging them to read your emails.

You grow, because what's the alternative? To stand still? To settle?

In fact, it isn't so much a question of if you should grow, rather how fast, how high, and when you should pull the trigger. Because growth and expansion means new staff; more staff; bigger premises; new machinery; massive risk; trips to the bank where you plead for millions, not thousands; expansion into new countries, and cultures, and industries. Growth is, and shall forever remain, one of the most dangerous minefields you encounter.

Which is wonderful, because for so long as you have the opportunity to grow, you're doing something right. The point is, though, if you get this wrong, it has the power to shock you and everything you've built up until this point. And although there are no flat-pack solutions to overcoming this issue, there are two aspects of growth that lead to mistakes more often than not: the first is to grow and expand for the wrong reason; the second is to do so too quickly. Both tend to intermingle and overlap with one another, but the true issue comes down to growing for the wrong reason, for which you must, once again, consider your judgment.

And this can sneak up and shock anyone, even experienced and famed entrepreneurs. Take Rachel Elnaugh, for instance, and the time she lost it all despite millions sitting in her bank account.

Famed for her time on the popular TV show, Dragon's Den, Rachel grew Red Letter Days into one of the UK's premier experience day and gift businesses. Meeting her at one of London's bustling business shows, I was somewhat nervous to come face-to-face with an entrepreneur who calls the likes of Richard Jones, Jeffrey Archer, and Donald Trump her friends.

'We were making millions in revenue,' she said, doing nothing to calm my nerves. 'This should have been a sign things were going well and not to change, but we went for broke, and I think it's here our mindset switched from what we could offer our customers, to how much money we could make from them.'

I interviewed Rachel rather early into this *Successful Mistake* adventure, so it shocked me to hear a successful person talk about growth and expansion in such a way. After all, she grew her business into one of the country's biggest, so she must have been rather good at it.

The thing is, there's a big difference between growing for the right reasons, versus the wrong ones, and it's Red Letter Days' growth and expansion during this period that kick-started the beginning of the end. It also led to one of the most devastating moments of shock I've seen.

'It was actually a massive relief when the business went into administration,' Rachel said, when I asked how she felt about losing the business she began from scratch. 'It was one of the worst things to ever happen to me, but, in reality, a massive burden lifted from my shoulders.'

You may struggle to comprehend this, as I'm sure you equate the loss of your business to a death in your family. But growing and expanding for the wrong reasons changed Rachel's role in Red Letter Days, how she saw her business, and how she felt about it.

'One of these changes was to bring in a CEO to replace me, which in hindsight was another mistake,' she said. 'Playing with, and changing a company culture is a dangerous game to play.'

After listening to Rachel describe the ultimate business hardship, it demonstrated how dangerous growth could be. Red Letter Days had money in the bank, and twelve years to its name, yet it still crumbled before her, all because she reached for more; more money, more market share, more customers.

If you never grow your business you'll fall behind and fail, but doing so for the wrong reason isn't the answer, either. Rachel's mistake came twelve years into the business, but a more common struggle is to grow in the early days, and in today's Internet age of viral fame and Silicon Valley investors, growing for the wrong reason — and doing so too quickly — produces devastating results.

Take Sam Tarantino, a man after my own heart; a music lover and creative thinker, and founder of Grooveshark, the online music streaming service that shares a market with the likes of Spotify, Pandora, and Soundcloud. Sam never had the luxury to sit back and grow with grace, and in a similar vein to Jon Crawford and StorEnvy, he fast-tracked almost everything he did.

'In 2010, it was all about growth,' he said, Skyping from Grooveshark HQ. 'We looked for new people and filled as many roles as we could, but it's like a tree with more branches than the trunk can hold. After a while, it snaps. Because we were growing for growth's sake, we didn't have people involved who loved the company. We didn't have the foundation or experience to handle it, so went from a high of 150 employees to a low of 40. By growing too fast, we hurt our growth by six months to a year.'

I suppose it's somewhat ironic to stifle your growth through growth itself, but in the same way that Red Letter Days grew owing to the pursuit of more, Grooveshark did so because they could. I mean, why not? When you have investment and exist in a competitive and thriving market, to grow is to be king, yes?

Well, as Sam shows, this isn't always the case.

It's tempting to grow at a pace, especially in a competitive landscape, but it's like building a house on a muddy field and skipping the foundations because your neighbours already have a few walls up. It's fine to extent, but before long your bricks and mortar shift and crack.

Sam watched Grooveshark's culture slip and slide, diluting the talented team he began with by introducing those who didn't belong. Dare I say his pursuit for growth led to a few hiring mistakes of his own, which shows how intermingled these attributes of mistakes are. One leads to another, and one's born from the last, and so it continues. And again, it comes down to your judgement and making the right decision instead of taking the easy one, the quick one, the one that seems like the right thing to do because everyone else does it.

Your business is your business! These are your decisions to make, and you make them to better the world you've built. If you're not growing or expanding for the right reasons, what else do you expect to happen?

It may sound strange to hear someone like Rachel talk about feeling relieved when her baby finally collapsed, but because she showed poor judgement and grew for the sake of growing, she fell out of love. She went through the motions and lost touch with why she had set up her business in the first place. And this can happen to anyone, at any stage, along their entrepreneurial adventure.

Now, none of this means you shouldn't grow or expand because your duty as an entrepreneur is to do just that.

Between now and the end of your days, you'll have the opportunity to grow and spread your wings, and so long as you do so for the right reasons, and you do it at a pace that won't destroy what you built in the first place, you'll do just fine. If you lose sight of this, you may set yourself up for a truly shocking moment. Because imagine how Rachel felt, not only losing her business, but feeling relieved when it happened. Consider the shock and pain that Sam went through when he had to fire over 100 people because he pushed too hard, too soon.

Just like with hiring, your business' growth hinges on your ability to show good judgement, which just so happens to lead us to our next attribute: decision-making.

After all, as an entrepreneur you're accountable to you and yourself, so your ability to make good decisions... Well, that's kind of important, don't you think?

INSPIRED BY STORIES FROM: RACHEL ELNAUGH, SAM TARANTINO, ARNOLD DU TOIT, JO DAVIES, DEAN PHILLIPS, DAVE HIRSKCHOP, JACOB HILL, TONY ABBOTT, ANDREW COOPER, BRIAN HORN

DECISION MAKING'S TRICKY DANGERS

Would you like to know one of the main aspects that drew me towards working for myself and leaping into this entrepreneurial madness?

Freedom.

The freedom to make my own decisions; to take my life and opportunities into my own hands and be the master creator who decides what is and isn't the right path to take.

You understand this, of course, because I'm sure these same needs drive you. But it isn't until you become an entrepreneur that you realise how much freedom you have. And how many decisions you need to make; how each day you face numerous crossroads that offer opportunity, possibility, failure, success, and every other conceivable outcome.

I imagine that the temptation to bite off more than you can chew forever remains with you, because I've spoken to entrepreneurs at various stages along their journeys who suffered at the mercy of decision-making; in particular when deciding when to say yes, and when to say no.

The ability to say no is arguably one of the most important skills you can learn because as an entrepreneur, opportunity and potential surrounds you each day. There's always a new idea, a new project, a new person and a new collaboration. There's always the temptation to try something new because maybe you aren't growing fast enough.

Or maybe you're growing, so you're tempted to diversify, take on more work and projects and stride into bigger and better markets.

In its most fundamental form, decision-making comes down to you saying yes or no, but as an entrepreneur it isn't when you say no that tends to be an issue, rather the frequency with which you say yes.

Take Ethan Austin, the co-founder of Give Forward: one of the first crowd-funding platforms to form in 2008, offering people and businesses an opportunity to crowd source their ideas and projects.

During a pre-Kickstarter age, Ethan and the Give Forward team said yes time and time again, eager to please every single person they could.

'In the early days we tried to be a platform for anyone and anything,' he said. 'In that first year we raised a total of $6,000 in revenue, realising that because we tried to be all things to all people, we didn't connect with anyone.'

That's a danger to any business at any time, but it's especially difficult for start-ups and fresh-faced entrepreneurs still finding their feet.

Before you know what your niche is, and who you can best serve, it's hard to say no. You love the idea of becoming an authority figure in a specific industry, but what if you choose the wrong one, or the small one, or the 'not quite ready yet' one. Such thoughts spiralled through Ethan's mind during Give Forward's infancy, but it wasn't until they honed in on a more specific market that they gained traction.

'We realised the people who loved our platform were those who used it for medical campaigns,' he continued. 'They were telling us and showing us what to do, but it took a while before we listened.'

Once they said no to marketing to everyone, and yes to a specific few, they grew and grew, and have now raised over $155 million for worthy campaigns and causes. Even though 'no' seems like a crazy word to say in business, it was this decision that set their growth in motion.

And when I sat down with my fellow Yorkshire entrepreneur, Tom Greveson, I heard about his similar pain after he'd said yes-yes-yes and tried to be everything to everyone. As the founder of

Revolution Viewing, an interactive video production company from Leeds, Tom built a high quality product that could potentially help a variety of businesses in an array of industries, and he targeted them all.

'I was a Jack-of-all-trades,' he said, 'I tried hard and showed enthusiasm, but wasted a lot of time and made a lot of wrong choices. I wasn't building anything, and if I'd carried on like that I'd still be a one-man band struggling to get by. The big turning point was when we built traction with our 360° tours, and realised if we focused on one market worth £100,000, and captured 15% of it, we'd be okay.'

Although this may not sound like a lot, it provided Tom with something to focus on, which in time grew organically as they realised who they could best serve. But this couldn't happen until he made the decision to say no to targeting everyone, and instead focus on the right someone.

I know simplifying your decision-making process into a single yes or no is rather idiotic, because life isn't so black and white. But when you think about it, each day you surround yourself with opportunity and possibility, and most of your decisions do come down to you either saying yes or saying no. As an entrepreneur, you're wired to say yes-yes-yes because it's here where opportunity and possibility lie.

But as my buddy Michael O'Neal from *The Solopreneur Hour* says, 'Say yes to opportunity, not to more work.'

We'll revisit Michael's inspiring story further into this journey, but it's important you appreciate his words now because they define how vital an entrepreneur's decision-making is. Your decision-making drives your judgement, which so many aspects of your business hinge upon. In fact, I've found it's rarely a product or service that forms long-lasting success, but instead the decisions made by those behind the products and services.

As an entrepreneur, it's the most powerful tool you possess. The moment you forget this is the moment you may invite impending shock into your life. Both Ethan and Tom struggled for far too long, not owing to bad luck or somebody else, but rather to the decisions they made — or didn't make, as the case may be.

Of course, it's difficult to know when to say yes and when to say no, although it's far easier if you appreciate what your passion and purpose is. It's these that keep you on the straight-and-narrow, but it's a fine balance indeed.

And it's good news for you, because it's what we focus on next. So, ready yourself for a passionate read and a group of people with real purpose driving them forward.

INSPIRED BY STORIES FROM: MICHAEL O'NEAL, CHRIS BROGAN, BRENTON HAYDEN, ETHAN AUSTIN, TOM GREVESON, LIAM PATERSON, TOM EWER, JIMMY VARLEY, DAVE URISLLO, CHRIS CERRONE, COLIN WRIGHT, DANNY INY, ALEXIS GRANT, BRIAN GARDNER, GARY BUTTERFIELD, HELEN TODD, JAMES EDER, OLLIE LEWIS, WILL TROTT

THE VALUE OF PASSION & PURPOSE

You've no doubt read about plenty of entrepreneurs building businesses around their passions, and how you should, too. I wouldn't disagree with this, but what I've found more important than passion itself is to ensure that it's aligned with purpose. Passion alone only takes you so far, and with so many daily tasks on your to-do list, it's easy to forget about what your passion is, what it means to you, and the reason it's your passion in the first place.

After all, isn't the biggest issue you face each day the maze of *stuff* that gets in your way and desires your attention right now — the emails, bookkeeping, networking, client work, your work, web work, social media, marketing... This daily grind steals your passion, and so often taints it.

That's why I want to turn your attention towards your purpose, because this not only focuses on what you enjoy and love, but also the value you can offer to others. Purpose requires a certain amount of vision, and makes you think about how you help and serve others, whereas passion concentrates on today and what *you* like.

It may be a small difference, but it's a significant one, and it was when I Skyped Dave Conrey, the founder of FreshRag, one late August evening, that I realised this.

'It can't just be passion driven, it has to have some sort of purpose,' he said, discussing his own journey from artist to art director. 'My passion is to help creative businesses, whereas my purpose is to help them see the world in a different light; helping them switch from a starving artist mindset, to an abundant artist one.'

Passion is what you love, but purpose is how you help others through this. Purpose forces you out of today, and ensures you consider who you serve and where you're going: tomorrow, next week, next year...

As an entrepreneur, you're tempted to focus on today, each and every day, because there's so much stuff to do, but if all you do is focus on right now, won't you spend the rest of your life reacting to circumstance? It's this reactive mindset that creates so many mistakes in the first place, so although passion matters, it's when you combine it with purpose that things really come together. The same can be said for purpose; this similarly only takes you so far, when considered in isolation.

When I logged on to speak to Jayson Gaignard, one of the finest 'connectors' in the world, and the mastermind behind *Mastermind Talks*, he didn't focus on his world of today — one he shares with the likes of Tim Ferris, AJ Jacobs, and James Altucher — but rather his previous life, where he made lots of money but never felt fulfilled.

'One of my biggest mistakes was starting a business for the wrong reasons; or should I say, picking the wrong business,' he said, describing his pre-*Mastermind Talks* existence where he founded a ticket-selling business which grew into Canada's third largest. As entrepreneurs, we're taught to pick our business based on opportunity and where the money is. Yet time and time again you hear about these people who begin a business at the expense of their health and relationships, and strive towards some financial goal, only to stop and say, "Now what?" when they eventually reach it.'

Jayson served a purpose because he genuinely helped people and started a thriving business, but, because he lacked passion, he became complacent and lethargic, racking up large amounts of debt in the process.

'To an extent, I had to sabotage myself,' he said, telling me about the end of his old life. 'I knew so long as I had Plan B — a business making money — I'd never follow through with Plan A — to create a company that lights me up.'

Which brings us back to passion, and creating a business around something that drives you and ignites your motivation like no other. After all, if you're to create a business that steals twelve hours of your day for the next fifty years, it may as well be something you're passionate about, right?

Absolutely, but with a long-lasting and undeniable *but*...

Because as we said earlier, passion alone only takes you so far, which Claud Williams found out the hard way. Today, Claud heads-up Dream Nation: a community of young and aspiring go-getters with the dream to not only change their own lives, but those they serve and surround. He's an inspiring young man, to say the least, but when I first met Claud he didn't quite have it all figured out.

'My biggest mistake was a slow burner,' he said, discussing the photography and videography business he started whilst still at university. 'Photography and videography is something I fell in love with, so the fact that I was able to do it as a job was a dream come true. But I put too much pressure on myself and tried to do everything on my own, and ultimately fell out of love with the camera. Even though I had a great summer, and made money, I had to quit photography. I dreaded the idea of picking up the camera, and once I realised I'd lost my passion, the money and growth meant nothing.'

You could argue that Claud had both passion and purpose, because he not only did something he loved, but had paying clients who wanted more of his services. Good times, right? Indeed, but only for so long as his passion and purpose balanced with one another.

When a new client knocks on your door, you say yes-yes-yes because your focus remains on now-now-now. Like Claud, you hustle and bustle like so many entrepreneurs do, until one day your passion evaporates into nothing. This is where the true danger lies when it comes to building a business on your passion, and I'd argue that although Claud did have the purpose to run alongside this, he didn't keep it balanced, focusing too much on the here and now.

'When you're down in the trenches running your business, it

stops you from seeing the big picture,' he said. 'When you neglect this, you simply take things as they come. These days I make sure I take a step back and think about where I am and where I'm heading.'

When it comes to you and your business, it's never a case of passion *or* purpose. The two need to sit side by side, aligned and balanced so you can grow and thrive. Purpose alone may fill your bank account with money and riches, but leave you somewhat unfulfilled and longing for more.

Passion alone only takes you so far too, for if you don't serve a real purpose, isn't what you have a hobby?

And even then, if these two important qualities do come together, it's important you keep them there because it's too easy to lose focus, get caught up in today; and like Claud, wake up one morning and dread the thought of picking up your camera.

Passion… Purpose… Too much… Too little… Each scenario leads to the same kind of mistake and pain.

It's balancing these two powerful entities that determines so much of your journey ahead: passion keeps your focus on today, so you love what you do and give it your all; purpose ensures you continue to serve tomorrow and beyond, proving real value to your customers and audience. It isn't one or the other, my friend, it's about inviting them both into your life, which I'm afraid to say is where many business owners fall short. Jayson did, as did Claud, and a number of other people I spoke to for this book. And if the thought of losing a grip on your passion scares you, or living the rest of your life unfilled despite having money in the bank, lucky for you we now tackle fear and how it affects even the most experienced and successful entrepreneurs.

INSPIRED BY STORIES FROM: JAIME MASTERS, ROSS KEMP, PAM SLIM, GREG HICKMAN, CLAUD WILLIAMS, DAN MILLER, CHRISTINE RICHMOND, JAYSON GAIGNARD, TEMI KOLEWO, TOM MORKES, SATI SALONA, TEMI KOLEOWO, TRENT DRYSMID, VERNON ROSS, JOANNA PENN

FEAR

I don't know about you, but my biggest fear in life is to get to seventy years old and look back with nothing but longing. You know, that dreaded feeling of 'what if', and all those experiences you could have had, but didn't because of time or circumstance. It's this fear that drove me to travel before university, work in America, get my Masters, and work for myself.

Without this fear I'd never have written my first novel. I suppose I wouldn't even write these words if it wasn't for my dreaded obsession over *what might be...*

As with mistakes and failure, you fear *fear*; but it's so often this fear that drives and motivates you to do what you do. Maybe you're like me and find it hard to determine between fear and excitement; two emotions that seem so entwined with one another.

The truth is, I didn't expect to come across fear a great deal during my interviews because I had this foolish thought that successful people somehow outgrew it or were above feeling scared and insecure.

You look at someone you admire and assume they're better than that.

They're stronger than you, right?

They're made of sterner stuff, yes?

No.

They're human, just like you are, and suffer with fear today like they did at the beginning of their journey.

So, although I believe that your fear motivates you, and has the power to bring out the best in you, it's important to respect how dangerous it is, too. Because if fear can hold someone like Debbie Millman back for over a decade, it can prevent you from fulfilling your dreams.

As President of Sterling Brands, Debbie's worked with some of the biggest organisations on the planet (Disney, IBM, Paypal, and Pepsi to name a few), and, considering she juggles her corporate life with book authorship and the popular podcast *Design Matters*, she's seen it all.

I anticipated an epic mistake involving one of her über clients, but instead she focussed on her self-doubt before any of this began.

'I looked deep into my future and panicked,' she said, describing her days, fresh out of university. 'I worried I wouldn't be able to look after myself or fulfil any of my dreams. At that moment I compromised,' she continued. 'I decided it was prudent to choose self-efficiency over my dreams and ambitions, to ensure I'd be secure. This isn't only tragic, but impossible. I figured "maybe if I wait until I'm more confident I'll be able to chase my dreams." But if all you do is wait for this to happen, you may end up waiting forever.'

Debbie's fear literally prevented her from beginning her journey in the first place, and although she refused to regret her time in the corporate world, the fact that she let fear dictate her path from the offset continues to leave a bitter aftertaste.

I wish I could say Debbie was alone in this, but she isn't, and it's scary to think how some of our favourite personalities and thought leaders nearly caved into fear's demands. Take Srinivas Rao, for instance, the mastermind behind the Unmistakable Universe (including *The Unmistakable Podcast*), and the guy who spent years chasing qualifications for no particular reason.

'I spent so much of my life chasing accolades, that I realised I didn't know how to do anything,' Srini said. 'This was a huge a-ha moment, because all I'd done was pursue meaningless metrics and pieces of paper.'

With a degree from Berkley, and an MBA from Pepperdine, Srini ticked all the boxes he assumed he had to tick, but the more we chatted, the more frustrated he grew. Where Debbie's fear and self-doubt had forced her to take the sensible corporate route, Srini had filled his resume with as much glory as possible, because… well, that's what you're supposed to do, right?

'I took part in what I call the ego-driven pursuit of what looks good on paper,' he continued. 'Looking back, I think I wanted the external accolades more then the work itself. And I wasn't happy. It's weird because you can go through life in this state, where it's like sleep walking and going through the motions. You don't realise you're unhappy because you're comfortable, but being comfortable is a dangerous position to be in.'

In the same way that fear prevented Debbie from starting and taking that all important risk, Srini's doubts refused to let him branch out, and place his best foot forward, because his mind remained fixed on the numbers and names, and for a while this followed him into the online world.

'I did this with my blog, too. In the beginning I was driven by the numbers and the type of guest I could get on the show. I still wanted the external accolades, and I got a few, too. I was named one of Probloggers' 'bloggers to watch' in 2011, but if I started out as one to watch, I certainly didn't end the year as one. But all this changed how I approach my work today, because I see what I do as more of an art form now. It's no longer numbers driven, or dictated by who has the biggest audience or biggest brand. I find the intrinsic value in everything I do, and work on, which I couldn't see before.'

Maybe you can relate to Debbie or Srini right now, and maybe your fear keeps you on some invisible fence where you're too afraid to do one or the other so you commit to nothing at all.

This is what your fear wants.

It tells you to wait a little longer until you're more experienced, have more money, or feel more settled… But there's no perfect period to bring meaning into your life.

And you're reading this book because you desire more. You wish to overcome your mistakes and failure because you refuse to let them define you. Your fear doesn't want you to do that. It doesn't want you to act, or be strong, it encourages you to hide and wait another day; just one more day…

If you choose to listen to fear, all you do is waste precious moments from your one and only life. This isn't just true for entrepreneurs, but for every person on the planet, because fear's a part of life. Maybe it's embedded deep within you as part of your fight or flight instinct, which make sense, I suppose, because who in their right mind would want to live the life of an entrepreneur? It's an insane journey to be on, so of course your fear keeps you at bay and wants you to take the easier option… the safer one.

But you must fight it and find your courage, because like Debbie said, referring to a conversation she'd had with Danni Shapiro, the bestselling author of books like *Slow Motion* and *Still Writing*, 'We think we need confidence to do something and take action, but confidence isn't what we need, as this often holds us back. What's more important than confidence is courage and competence.'

Courage and competence, not confidence…

Once Debbie shared this with me, I smiled because when fear strikes, how confident do you tend to feel? If you're anything like me you feel low and helpless, which means fear is doing its job, tempting you to quit, or stop, or never begin in the first place. Feeling afraid and full of self-doubt doesn't make you weak or incapable of acting, achieving, *doing*. It means you're human and scared of the unknown, which is fine because you don't need confidence, merely to find a little courage and belief in your competencies.

All this brings us back to this notion that fear has the power to both cripple you and motivate you. It's not that successful people like Debbie and Srini regret their time in the corporate world or at school, because such periods are part of their journey and who they are. What frustrates them — the reason they look back and consider it a mistake — is that they allowed fear to hold them back.

They let their fear cripple them instead of motivate them. They did what they thought they had to do instead of what they needed to. They lost precious moments that they'll never get back, and delayed their inevitable success, and you – You! Reading these words! – you don't have time for that.

Fear's part of your journey. It comes with every new idea, project, venture, and partnership you form. You'll doubt yourself and feel insecure, and you'll have plenty of opportunity to give into this fear or turn it into your greatest motivation.

I hope you choose the latter, because when folk like Debbie and Srini shared their greatest mistake, I sensed their frustration and longing to have those lost moments back.

With this, we approach the end of these attributes and touch upon our next; communication. You don't need me to tell you how important communication's role is, although what I'm about to share may surprise you.

INSPIRED BY STORIES FROM: DEBBIE MILLMAN, JEN GRESHAM, NATALIE SISSON, SRINIVAS RAO, OMAR ZENHOM & NICOLE BALDINU, JOHN LEE DUMAS, MOE ABDOU, SATI SALONA

COMMUNICATION: IT'S GOOD TO TALK

One of your most important jobs as an entrepreneur is to communicate effectively at all times. That's easier said than done, because communication's realm is neither small nor simple. So, before we get into the nitty gritty of the mistakes that arise from poor communication, let's consider a few of the aspects you need to think about when it comes to communicating effectively.

For starters, you have a lot of people to communicate with; staff, customers, partners, suppliers, investors, the press, potential leads… And that doesn't even cover your personal relationships.

Then, of course, you must decide whether to talk or listen, how much to talk or listen, and when, how and what it is you intend to say. It's a complex beast, so you shouldn't be surprised to learn that poor communication results in a lot of big mistakes, in one form or another.

Personally, I always figured that it's how you communicate with your customers and audience that's the most important aspect of all, and so long as you ticked this box, everything else would slip into place. I also believed effective communication taught you a great deal about others (your staff, customers, industry and competitors), but I was proven to be wrong on both counts.

That's not to say communicating with your audience isn't vital, because all forms of communication are important, and I don't want you to think any other way about it after reading what's to come. But a vast majority of big business mistakes result from poor in-house communication — between co-founders, key suppliers, your staff, and investors — and it leads to fundamental issues that can affect the very nature of what you're building.

Take Brian Foley, for instance, the co-founder of BuddyTruk (an Uber-esque business transforming the process of moving house), and the story he told me about turning his app idea into app reality. The moment Brian told me about BuddyTruk, I knew he was onto a winner because my gut reaction was to say, 'why hasn't anybody already thought of this?'

After all, we don't all own trucks or have the ability to move beds and such, but we all tend to move house from time to time. Bridging this rather clear gap in the market... Well, it's safe to say that Brian and his team were on to a solid idea. But because Brian and his co-founders didn't have the necessary skills to build the app themselves, they had to outsource the development of it to a third party, and it's here where Brian learned the true importance of communication.

'We fell short of communicating what we wanted,' he said, from his Santa Monica home. 'We didn't necessarily need to know all the technical ins and outs about making an app, but we did need to know enough to articulate our vision to the developers, and ensure we remained on the same page throughout. For the longest time we blamed them when things went wrong, but it was our fault because we didn't know what we wanted. We didn't communicate our vision or plans with them; at least, not well enough.'

This resulted in a difficult period for Brian and his team, because they were left with a sub-par app that didn't meet their standards. They had this great idea, but couldn't turn it into a reality. And, although Brian's mistake demonstrated a clear lack of in-house conversation between co-founders and staff, it also hinted at a lack of effective communication between Brian and his partners.

'We knew if we didn't fix things soon, it wouldn't be a developer problem, but rather a vision one,' he said. 'We also realised that if everyone on our team had the same vision and worked towards the same goal, we couldn't fail.'

Brian talked about having to start again, literally scrapping the project and going back to day zero.

'It was hard to start again, but we ended up with a great product; one far better than we imagined — but only after articulating what we wanted with our developers. The thing is, it took us receiving an app that we didn't like before we realised what this was; let alone how vital communication is in order to achieve this.'

The moral of this tale is that although communication, in all forms, remains fundamental to you and your business, it's a lack of clear in-house communication that so often leads to your biggest mistakes and failures; not because of the wasted time, or money, or resources, but rather the danger of misunderstanding what your actual vision is.

It's one thing to have a great idea and to be able to chat about it for hours on end within your inner circle, but quite a different matter to then articulate this vision with your staff, investors, customers, suppliers, potential audience, and everyone else you wish to connect with.

You have to ask yourself; is an idea only real, so long as it remains in your head, or does it become reality once you involve other people and are able to articulate it to the world? I'd argue it's the latter, and once Brian and his co-founders faced this bigger picture issue head-on, communicated with each other and developed their purpose and vision, they were able to articulate this with the rest of their team. They were able to get them on the same page, remain on the same page, and create a far better app than they could have ever imagined.

Of course communicating with your customers is important, as is how effective you communicate your message with every other person who comes across you and your business. You must learn to both listen and talk, and develop the skill of knowing when to say what and how. But, I would argue that none of this matters unless you get that in-house communication sorted. Like Brian said, 'We knew if we didn't fix things soon, it wouldn't be a developer (product) problem, rather a vision one...'

That's why it's a lack of in-house communication that leads to the most devastating mistakes and failures, because fixing a product is one thing, but fixing a vision creates an entirely different kind of hurdle to overcome. As such, communication's true value doesn't lie in the act of speaking or listening to others, nor how it teaches you more about these other people, but rather the way it helps you better understand what it is you want, who it is you are, and why it is you're on this journey.

This doesn't make every other facet of communication unimportant, but it renders them next to useless, unless you get the bigger picture sorted out first. With the subject of communication now covered, we're almost ready to move onward and upward along this successful mistake journey; but before we do, it's vital that you appreciate how not all mistakes are your fault, but how this also doesn't make a damn difference to the journey you're on.

INSPIRED BY STORIES FROM: LAURA BENSON, RON HOLT, NAOMI TIMPERLY, MARY JUETTEN, BRIAN FOLEY, MATT CHEAVRONT, LINDSEY RAINWATER & STEVE OLSHER, MATT CHEUVRONT, CLAIRE MORLEY JONES, CC CHAPMAN, NEIL PATEL

EXTERNAL ISSUES: IT'S NOT ALWAYS YOUR FAULT

You've just read about six key attributes that make up the mistakes that entrepreneurs like you make all too often, and the common dominator so far is you: your decisions, your fear, your passion and purpose, your communication.

It's time to throw a spanner in the works, because sometimes you're held prisoner by a shocking mistake made by someone else. Maybe an employee or business partner messes up and leaves you to clean up the chaos. Maybe it's an external PR issue that you're pulled into, owing to a supplier or customer. Maybe it's property related, or a decision made out of your hands. There are numerous mistakes that others can make that can affect you in the same way as if you make the mistake yourself.

This sucks, hurts and most certainly isn't fair, but the buck stops with you. You're the one who chose to partner with said co-founder, hire said employee, involve yourself in said industry.

We'll look more at blaming yourself or others, and how pointless it is to do so, shortly.

It's easier said than done, I know, but external issues that are out of your control do happen, and when they do, you have to push through it like you would any other mistake or failure, *be it yours or not*. And there's one such issue that every single one of us is at the mercy of, which is not only difficult to overcome, but near impossible to plan for. I refer, of course, to that dreaded word 'recession'. It doesn't have to be a recession per se; rather any political, economical, or environmental situation you cannot control.

I've heard one too many stories about an entrepreneur who has worked hard, found success, and built his or her empire, only to watch it slip through their fingers as bankers destroy the system from the inside out, or for Mother Nature to leave nothing in her wake.

Take Desiree East, an artist and creative coach who owned a thriving landscaping business with her husband in 2009. Although she didn't work directly in the real estate industry, it didn't prevent the rug from being pulled out from under her world when the entire system imploded.

'It was hit hard along with the housing market,' she told me, Skyping from the sunny west coast of America. 'We hit rock bottom. The calls stopped. The money ran dry. We had this amazing house we loved, but because of the recession we had to let it go. We sold half of our possessions and downsized. It was a huge change, and a devastating time to live through.'

I remember my call with Desiree and trying to pinpoint a mistake her husband and she made, but I couldn't. Such external issues affect all of us, no matter what your business and industry. You can prepare to an extent and save for a rainy day, but there's only so much you can plan for.

'Even though this mistake wasn't our fault, we still went through the process of blaming ourselves, asking what we could do differently, and so on,' she said.

Stories like Desiree's are tough to listen to because it's one thing owning up to a mistake you made, but another when it's down to someone else. Yet in many ways this is the perfect way to end this particular section of the book, because it demonstrates its entire point; mistakes happen.

As you work your way through the rest of these seven stages, you'll learn how to spot your mistakes; how to overcome them, what you need to do in order to transform them into success, and yes, to an extent, avoid them in the first place. But you'll never rid your world of mistakes and failure altogether.

No matter how experienced, wealthy, and talented you may be, or may become, mistakes remain part of your equation, and although many of your faux pas will be down to you, some will not.

They may be owing to someone else, or a series of external events you cannot control, but here's the most important thing that you can remember right now… Whether your mistakes and failures are your fault or not, they remain yours to deal with. It's up to you to transform this bad time into a good one, and it's you who will suffer through the pain and the shock and everything else. But this is fine, because it's also you who reaps the lessons learnt from your 'once upon a time' hardship.

So, as you read the rest of this book, appreciate that not all your mistakes will be down to you, and accept this, because you're the one who still gets to enjoy the juicy rewards at the end of stage seven.

Yes, the shock hurts, and when you're in the moment it feel all the more brutal when you know it isn't because of you but someone else, a different business, or indeed some banker who decided to rip the economy apart from the inside. It's up to you to take a breath and own it nevertheless, and ensure you guide yourself through all those stages, all the way to the promised land at the end of stage seven.

However, let's not get ahead of ourselves just yet, because we're not quite though Stage One: Shock, and although most of your mistakes and failures revolve around one or more of these seven attributes, more often than not, there are warning signs that shine on your 'soon to be' mistake before it has chance to ignite. So, as we leave the attributes of a mistake to one side, let's focus on the warning signs that so often precede them, because the sooner you appreciate what these are, the sooner you can overcome your mistakes, and indeed, avoid them in the first place.

INSPIRED BY STORIES FROM: TEA SYLVESTER, DESIREE EAST, CORBETT BARR, MARK SEAMEN, ANDREW HELM, KRISTIN THOMPSON, NICK UNSWORTH, STEWART ROSS, JASON GRACIA

THE WARNING SIGNS: WHEN TEDIUM STRIKES, TAKE NOTE

Although this book focuses on an array of inspiring entrepreneurs, it's as if this section was designed for me. When it comes to tedium and growing bored of a new project — forever striding for the new idea, better idea, fresher idea — I'm an absolute nightmare. The fact that I committed to this book is a miracle in itself, but I'm not the only one to suffer at tedium's feet because when it comes to warning signs you should take note of, boredom leads the way.

That's not to say it's a sign of a bad idea or your cue to run away, because that leads to its own issues. After all, if I'd quit as soon as I grew bored of writing this book, I'd never have written it. Writing has its painful moments, just like your own work does. Although sometimes tedium is a signal to run and quit, on other occasions it's your cue to persist and keep your course.

It's often difficult to determine which instinct to follow, but a successful approach towards boredom is to reflect on where you are and what you're doing, because if anything else a mistake may be near. Tedium breeds poor judgment, you see; when you're bored, you eat crap you shouldn't. When you're bored, you waste hours watching awful TV. When you're bored, you end up texting your ex and beginning a conversation you're bound to regret.

We've all been there. It's a bad time, and as we already discussed, poor judgement and business don't play nicely with one another. There happens to be two people I know, both who suffered at the hands of tedium, but in rather different ways. Where Alexandra Franzen's boredom taught her to change course, Thomas Frank persisted with his idea and committed to it outright. We'll get to Alexandra in a moment, but first let's introduce you to Mr Frank, and how he had too much time on his hands without enough work to fill it.

When he set up College Info Geek, whilst studying at university,

Thomas focused on his writing and blogging, helping his fellow students to deal with the hardships of loans, budgeting, and the like.

'My mistake was actually making my life too simple,' he said, describing the period after his blog gained traction and began to boom. 'When I started college, I filled as much time as I could with club duties, becoming an RA in my dorm, and getting a part-time job. I started College Info Geek on the side, but once it began to grow I decided to cut everything else from my life that wasn't essential.'

'My thought process,' he continued. 'Was that now I had all this extra time, I'd be able to get more work done'. But as the semester went on, I did less work than ever because when you give yourself a ton of unstructured time, it's easy to spend it unwisely.'

Listening to his story, I nodded in agreement, empathising with each word, because I too grow bored and lazy as a project develops. But Thomas' boredom wasn't down to his idea, but rather to the excess of time tempting him to eat this, watch that, and text one ex after the other.

In other words, he grew complacent.

Complacency is one of your biggest obstacles, because how productive are you when bored and lethargic? I know I'm not, and I've met few people who thrive in such circumstances.

Thomas slipped into tedium's rut, not because he didn't enjoy College Info Geek, or that it was a bad idea, but because he lost sight of what he had built due to having few deadlines to meet.

As he said himself, 'Our brains like to have a deadline.'

So instead of walking away from his business, he refocused and found accountability and purpose.

But on the other hand, sometimes tedium's warning sign is telling you to walk away from an idea altogether, which

Alexandra Franzen found after slipping into a rut during the early days of her business.

As a prolific writer of books like *50 Ways To Say You're Awesome*, Alexandra honed in on one of her skillsets early, offering a specific yet required service to her clients.

'When I launched my business in 2010, I tried to "niche" myself too quickly,' she said. 'I positioned myself as a creative resumé and cover letter writer — something that I was not only good at, but a service people wanted.

'In reality, this wasn't my life's calling. It was too limiting and the work grew very tedious, very quickly. So I switched gears and repositioned myself as a writer and storyteller for entrepreneurs. With this shift, I could breathe again and had room to grow and attract the kind of clients I desired.'

In contrast to Thomas, Alexandra filled her time with paying work and eager clients, but because she focused on something that didn't light a fire within her, tedium struck and held her prisoner. I sense she suffered the same disillusion and complacency as Thomas, for rather different reasons. But rather than persist and refocus, Alexandra needed to reposition her entire business and approach.

Resumé writer wasn't a bad idea per se, but it was a bad idea for her, and the fact that she suffered through each boring day provided her with all the warning she needed. As an entrepreneur, you will grow bored of projects and ideas and certain aspects of your work. This alone doesn't mean you should walk away or quit, but it's a sure sign to take a step back and reflect. And maybe you're not bored of a particular task or project. Maybe it's something much grander than this. Maybe it's actually a sign that you've fallen out of love with your work altogether, or you aren't doing what you need to.

Tedium and boredom alone don't provide an answer, but they are a signal to reflect, and ask yourself, 'Why the hell am I so bored?'

Tedium breeds poor judgement, remember, so if you ignore it, or rush into rash decisions, a potential mistake may hide around the corner. Don't react, or brush it under the carpet, instead take note and consider why you're bored, frustrated, or underwhelmed in the first place. The answer may be to quit, but, equally, it may be to persist by refocusing, tweaking, or changing a little of this and a pinch of that. Either way, growing bored of what you do isn't a mistake on its own, but if you leave to it grow and rumble out of control, that moment of shock maybe closer than you think.

So, if you find yourself bored and lethargic, take a peek within and ask yourself why. Which brings us to the next warning sign on your horizon, and the role your gut instinct plays when a mistake is near.

INSPIRED BY STORIES FROM: ALEXANDER FRANZEN, THOMAS FRANK, JIM HOPKINSON, DAVE CONREY, NICK SIMMS, MITCH JOEL

HOW TO LISTEN TO YOUR GUT'S INNER WISDOM

An entrepreneur has many lessons to learn along the way, and no doubt one of the biggest you'll come across is when to listen to your gut. The problem with this is, what the hell does it mean?

Your gut instinct differs to the person's next to you, and there's no way to measure such a vague and overused term. But despite the fact I hate the cliché, 'listen to your gut', it provides one of the biggest warning signs in your journey ahead.

Maybe some aspects of life cannot be explained with a simple definition.

It seems to me that the whole notion of what is and isn't part of your gut's inner instinct fits into this category, so instead of trying to explain what it is, and how to find it, let's instead focus on why it matters: turning to AJ Leon — one of the most inspiring guys I know, and the chap who wrote this book's foreword — to guide you on your way.

Today, AJ runs Misfit Inc, along with his wonderful wife, Melissa. A group of forward-thinking brands, Misfit includes a publishing house, annual conference, digital agency, foundation, and an incubator under its umbrella. It's forever growing and pushing the boundaries and is famed for its artisan and quirky approach. Misfit employees live dotted around the world, and AJ and Melissa are literal nomads who spend one month here, another month there.

You may ask why I share this with you. Well, not long ago, AJ sat in a Wall Street corner office with the comfort of a large salary and those well-known bonuses you'll no doubt have heard of. A few weeks before his wedding, his boss offered him the promotion of a lifetime; flush with a bigger office, bigger salary, and enough security and comfort to keep him in fancy clothes until his end of days. Yet during this moment, that so many people dream about, AJ quit. He walked away. Something within him stopped him giving the obvious answer of yes, and this is the only way a simple man like myself can explain what your gut instinct is.

'As I walked back into my office, I looked out to the New York skyline and cried,' said AJ, whilst I interviewed him in front of a small gathering in my hometown of Sowerby Bridge. 'I felt trapped. For the first time, I realised I was living somebody else's life. I'd always dreamed of, one day, doing something purposeful, but I knew in that moment that if I took this promotion, I'd never walk away. The money and everything that came with it was too big. If I accepted, my dream was dead.'

Having spent much of his young adult life chasing money and degrees that offered the best return on his investment, AJ stood at a crossroads between the man he was, and the man he dreamed of being. He knew he had this desire to live a more purposeful life — one that didn't revolve around money — and he knew he wasn't on the right track to achieve this. He knew, deep down, he'd become the type of guy he didn't want to become.

The money and promotions and swanky Manhattan dinners tempted him, yet something within him shouted *no*. This is why your gut instinct matters, because it warns you about instants you don't trust. Will it always be right? Probably not. Will it always be clear and make sense? Almost never. But if it speaks, it speaks for a reason.

'If I hadn't left at that exact moment, I'd would have continued to be that guy for the rest of my life,' AJ said.

It's easy to look at AJ and say he made the right decision, but at the time he was leaping into the unknown mere weeks before his wedding. In my opinion, it takes a brave individual to listen to your gut during a time like this, and although we're all capable of such bravery, it maybe a step too far for most. What if your gut's wrong? What if you're the kind of person who doubts everyone and everything? What if it seems to jump between yes and no, driving you insane as it does?

Enter Evo Terra, the founder of Podiobooks, and a guy with one of the most eclectic business portfolios you'll meet. As we spoke on a crackly Skype call, he told me about an old client of his.

'I just *knew* this startup was doomed,' he said. 'It smelled bad from the beginning, but because I was a consultant and he paid me, everything was fine. But then after six months, he asked me to join, and even though I knew it was doomed to fail, I looked at the guy and saw someone who placed all his eggs in one basket. He had to make it work, so I thought, "Maybe I'm wrong... maybe I don't know this will fail, after all." Well, three months later, we ran out of money and I was out of a job, so maybe I should have trusted my instincts and ran as far away as possible.'

It's the keyword '*knew*' that illustrates the issue, because Evo didn't *know* it would fail, but something within him fired out the warning shots anyway. It isn't about saying yes or no, or a question of listening to your gut , because sometime it's right and other times it isn't.

On this occasion, Evo's gut was right, but he didn't listen. Whereas my good friend Chris Sands — who helped design this book's cover — once sat in a meeting with the infamous Tony Wilson of Factory Records *(the man who brought the world Joy Division, New Order, and The Happy Mondays)*, and said no, because his gut insisted.

'I'm on to something big,' said Tony. 'It's called an MP3, and in a few years it'll be huge.'

After listening for a few minutes, Chris scoffed. 'This is a terrible idea, Tony. It'll never catch on.'

A few years later the iPod came out and the rest is history, which goes to show your gut isn't always correct (in Chris' case, not by a long shot). But it isn't about yes or no; listening or not, it's about taking it as the warning sign it is.

'There isn't a brain within your gut,' said Evo, midway through our conversation. 'It doesn't do a great job of making decisions for you, so rather than make a snap judgement, I like to give myself time so my brain can create a more informed decision.'

I have no idea what constitutes a gut instinct, and I'm sure yours differs to mine. There's no way to measure it or create an out-of-the-box solution of whether to listen to it or not, but if your gut speaks, it does so for a reason, so you may like to listen to it, sleep on it, sit on it, and give your brain time to digest it. It's a mere warning sign of a potential mistake ahead, and who knows you better than your subconscious? Well, come to think of it, keeping yourself to yourself isn't always what it's cracked up to be...

INSPIRED BY STORIES FROM: EVO TERRA, GREG SMUK, AJ LEON, CHRIS SANDS, ALEXIS GRANT, CHARLIE KEMP, LUKE HODSON, MITCH JOEL, CC CHAPMAN, SEAN PLATT

TREAD WITH CARE WHEN ON YOUR OWN

Your life as an entrepreneur can become rather lonesome. With the long hours and travel, it's easy to isolate yourself within your own thoughts and ideas. Take me, for instance; a guy who writes and works in coffee shops ninety percent of the time, but who goes days without properly speaking to anyone — baristas aside.

You may surround yourself with co-founders and employees and technical folk, so you needn't worry about alienating yourself, right? Not necessarily, because when I talk about taking care when on your own, I don't literally mean being on your own. You can speak to one hundred people each day and still slip into isolation, because it isn't about how many people you speak to, rather who and how.

Surrounding yourself with staff and partners and family only takes you so far. I don't wish to devalue these groups of people by any means, but a true warning sign blinks to life when you trap yourself in your own little bubble. I don't care who you are because everyone's guilty of this from time to time, and it happens to fast track you to the front of mistake-hood's line. Like it did for Fraser Doherty when he spent over a year perfecting his brand with his ideas. Or John Corcoran, who woke up one day and realised that he'd spent so much time in his own mind, that he'd allowed the relationships he'd built up over the years to slip by the wayside.

We'll get to Fraser and John in a second, but the point to drum home is the need to escape your head — and when I say your head, I don't mean in a literal sense. For you, this may include a business partner or staff; close friends or family who struggle to share the whole truth; or mentors who may have your best interests at heart, but don't appreciate your customer or end user.

I suppose the takeaway from this is to tread with care if you slip into one of these micro-bubbles, but don't take my word for it. Take Fraser Doherty's, the young entrepreneur who transformed his grandma's jam recipe into a bona fide business at the age of sixteen. Aged twenty-four when I spoke to him, Fraser shared his teenage story and how it began in his parent's humble kitchen.

After a couple of years selling his jam in and around school, Fraser had the opportunity to showcase his brand to one of the UK's largest supermarkets, but not all went according to plan.

'Waitrose held a "meet the buyer" day,' he said, fresh-faced and sitting in his Belgian hotel room. 'Wearing my dad's suit, I pitched my idea after working on the packaging and brand for over a year. 'They turned me down there and then, and I won't lie, Waitrose saying "no" was one of the lowest parts of my journey so far. I learnt that the people you have to listen to are the customers themselves. They said no, but offered me valuable advice, so I went home and threw everything in the bin so I could start from scratch.'

Fraser had the support of family and friends, a loyal group of local customers, and even reached out to a local design company to help bring his vision to fruition. But none of this mattered because he had forgotten about his end user, who, in this instance, weren't just the consumers who bought it, but the supermarkets who stocked it.

'There's no point in hiring them unless you let them do their job,' he said, describing his relationship with the designer. 'It feels like your baby and it's hard to hand over control, but once you hire them you have to let them do their job.'

It's not that Fraser's idea was bad, as he shared his vision of a comic-book theme aimed at making people laugh and smile. I personally loved the idea, and you may, too, but the issue arose from Fraser's insistence to focus on his idea instead of seeking the advice of buyers, distributors, and those who deal with brands like these each day.

Fraser got lost within himself, and if you're honest with yourself, you'll realise you may have done this, too. I know I have, and my friend John Corcoran has, losing sight of the incredible relationships he built whilst working in the White House, Silicon Valley, and Hollywood.

Today, John owns a popular blog and podcast, is a writer and course builder, and one of the finest connectors I know — his little black book is the envy of the entrepreneurial world. Yet, having dedicated his working life to building relationships in the political and entertainment industries, John lost sight of this when crafting his own brand.

'I was building an online presence and blogging a great deal,' he said, sitting in front of a picture of him shaking Bill Clinton's hand. 'But my biggest mistake was failing to develop relationships with others in support of this journey. In the previous industries I'd worked in, I knew the importance of connecting with people, but in the early days of my own business I didn't build relationships with fellow bloggers, podcasters, and those working on their own online brand. As a result my growth stagnated, and I didn't go anywhere for a while.'

John got lost within himself, a common trap that many entrepreneurs fall into, focusing on his work, his writing and his brand. Before he knew it, several months had passed him by with very little to show for it. It isn't that your work or ideas aren't important, or that you should spend every waking moment at dreary networking events, but it's vital to escape the bubble you create for yourself.

'My lightbulb moment came when I took a course and was asked to write down a list of people who would help me if I launched a new product the next day. I realised that I had a list of about three, and no real network to claim. I'd built strong relationships in every job I had up until this point, except when it came to my own online brand.'

This lightbulb moment set John on a new path, focusing his attention on connecting and nurturing relationships with those around him. And, as someone with an enviable little black book, it's a pivotal moment that paid off.

John and Fraser both got lost within themselves, albeit in rather different ways. Where Fraser forgot to include his end user, John left opportunity on the table by forgoing relationships with like-minded bloggers and podcasters et al. That's not to say you shouldn't work on your own or, indeed, lose yourself within your bubble, because as an entrepreneur you will; you arguably sometimes need to.

You should also believe in your ideas and back yourself, but if you take a step back and have to admit you haven't included your end user — or have but haven't listened to them — then it's a sure sign to stop and smell the roses. And if you happen to write a list of your allies *(not including your close friends or family)* and cringe at how small the number is, then that's another warning sign that bad times await.

During my chat with Mr Corcoran, he mentioned an African Proverb that's rather apt for this stage of the book:

> 'If you want to go fast, go alone. If you want to far, go together.'

I'm personally a firm believer that you're capable of creating a good product on your own, but if you want it to be great then you must involve other people; your customers, your peers, your competitors, strangers. But in the same vein, it's important to beware of what others bring to your table, because as dangerous as losing yourself within yourself can be, being surrounded with a bunch of yes men leads to a different kind of terrible.

INSPIRED BY STORIES FROM: FRASER DOHERTY, JOHN CORCORAN, MARS DORIAN, GRANT BALDWIN, JOSH SPRAGUE, MARK MANSON, MATT CHEUVRONT

BEWARE OF THE YES MEN

One of main reasons I work for myself is because I made a terrible yes man. My old bosses would say they wanted me to speak my mind and that they surrounded themselves with those who pushed them and made their business better, but in reality they didn't like it.

I suppose, if I'm honest I don't like it; and you probably don't, either, After all, who likes folk who say no to you? I suppose a few do, but successful people tend to insist upon it.

We've already covered the power of no, so it shouldn't surprise you that an ever-present yes offers potential disaster. Having spoken to entrepreneurs who found themselves surrounded by yes men, it's something you may like to avoid. I know, I know, it feels great having people agree with you. It also feels great to say yes to others, again and again, because their faces light up and they hand you lots of lovely money. It's easy to say yes, and even easier to hear it, but if there's one thing that leads to failure, it's placing blind faith in the word.

For instance, let me introduce you to Brenton Hayden, the founder of Renters Warehouse: one of America's fastest growing and best reviewed property management companies. Brenton grew Renters Warehouse into one of America's largest, but not before suffering a few setbacks along the way. Chatting to me from his office, he told me about the early days and how he got all googly-eyed over the big client. Despite having a proven process that worked, and pleased his exiting customers, he wanted to please the 'big apples' now knocking on his door. He wanted to say yes. He wanted to have them part of his ever-growing portfolio.

'The big clients wanted to do business with me,' he said. 'I kept saying yes to them because we were a young business and they offered huge potential and big contracts. But I lost sight of what our business was built on, and instead focused too much on the top and bottom line. We changed the way we did things just for them, and we weren't good at it because we moved away from the proven process we'd worked hard to build.'

Although this happened during Brenton's early days, it's an issue that remains with an entrepreneur forever, because there's always a 'big apple' to be had.

There's always the temptation to say 'yes' to someone because of the potential they offer, but as Brenton says, 'Don't be clouded by the big client.' Not only does becoming a yes man take you away from what you're good at, it tempts you into making bad decisions.

Whilst all this was going on with Brenton, these so-called big clients vetted him and made sure he could deliver what he promised.

'They kept me so busy with background checks, that I forgot to do my own on them,' he said. 'Well, it turned out some of these big clients were bad apples indeed, and when their own issues came to light in 2008, we got tied into their mess and it affected our reputation.'

All this doesn't mean you should say no and only no, or turn down the chance of working with a big client because they push you and challenge you. But the moment you start saying 'yes' to everything you should worry, because not only does it take you away from what you're good at, but it also blinds you. And as dangerous as becoming a yes man is, surrounding yourself with other yes men presents equal danger.

Take Scott Oldford, the man behind INFINITUS, and one of the most committed and selfless individuals I've met along this journey. Today, Scott works with ambitious entrepreneurs to grow their businesses with effective funnels and unique online marketing communications, but as he offered a peek into his early years — when most of us are plucking up the courage to ask that girl or guy to the dance — he took my breath away with how quickly your world can crumble to pieces.

'I won around fourteen awards over a two year period,' Scott said, referring to his mid-teens when he began programming, building a thriving reputation, and forming a successful business from nothing. 'This wasn't a good thing, because when you have so many people saying you're great at a young age, you begin to believe it.'

Removing age from the equation, this remains dangerous for every type of entrepreneur. Whether people say yes to your idea, fawn over every word you say, or bow at your feet, believing this hype and surrounding yourself with people who say yes-yes-yes takes you down a potentially disastrous road.

'I think it's good to know you're good at something, but not to believe you're the best. This only made me cocky and egotistical, and ultimately created a monster; Scott Oldford, the monster.'

In the same way that saying 'yes' to your clients makes it hard to keep sight on what matters to you, having others say 'yes' to everything you utter, blurs the lines, too. Because let's face it, when have you ever come up with the perfect idea, implemented a plan to perfection, or perfected a process to a point where Zeus himself would kneel before you?

Scott surrounded himself with yes men at a young age, and it may have affected his personal life as much as his business one, but the point is to not underestimate how dangerous the word 'yes' can be.

'I learnt how quickly you can burn money,' Scott said, discussing the debt he racked up. 'I slipped to my lowest point, going from a complete success story to an utter failure.'

Oh sure, what a wonderful word yes can be and how easy it is to say. I love to hear it, too, and I'm certain you do as well, but it's a word that often creates nothing but short-term happiness with hints of delusion.

'No', on the other hand, keeps you humble.

I appreciate it's often a horrible word to hear, and a difficult one to say, but those two letters are vital in every entrepreneur's arsenal. So, if you find yourself saying 'yes' to a particular client when you feel you should be saying no, take a step back and reflect. If you're surrounded by a bunch of people singing your praises, who make you feel indestructible, take a damn step back and reflect. You may feel great right now because that's the power of *yes*. But it may not last for long.

And whilst on the subject of others and the blurred lines they can offer, it's a good time to move on to the next section and how too many people often confuse matters. The opinions of others may be a marvellous thing indeed, but the moment you listen to too many, you need to yet again   take note and reflect on where you are and what you're doing.

INSPIRED BY STORIES FROM: ETHAN AUSTIN, BRENTON HAYDEN, CHARLIE WILD, ERIN BLASKIE, LISA HAGGIS, NEIL PATEL, SCOTT OLDFORD, DANA HUMPHREY, DORIE CLARK

WHEN TOO MANY COOKS SPOIL THE PAD THAI

We've looked at the potential dangers of working on your own, but that doesn't mean that surrounding yourself with others brings nothing but joy. Folk say 'too many cooks spoil the broth', but too many entrepreneurs in a room create far greater chaos. Yet it isn't the overcrowding of co-founders and team members that seems to create issues, rather the point when you surround yourself with too many people, too many voices, and too many opinions in general.

It's important to listen to others and form ideas that go beyond your own, but it's vital that you control this and ensure you only involve the right people at all times. Let's revisit our friend from earlier, Rachel Elnaugh. Many of her problems arose when she listened to other people who said she should hire a new CEO, grow the business, do this, and do that.

The action of listening to all these voices should have been all the warning she needed, because not long after her business and livelihood slipped through her fingers. If you find yourself listening to a lot of people who want to share lots of ideas — enticing you to take this path or that one— it's a sign to step back and reflect on what it is they're actually saying. It's what Steve Olsher wished he'd done back in the nineties when the early Internet was all the rage. Steve's one of today's experts on reinvention and helping people to find their inner calling, as well as the author of *What is Your What*. But if you rewind back to the last century, Steve lived another life altogether.

'We were convinced, hook, line and sinker, by our investment bankers that in order to reach the promised land, Wall Street would want seasoned executives at the helm,' Steve said, discussing his first major business venture, Liquor.com.

Having grown his online business before the dotcom boom, reaping the benefits once everything took off, Steve had plenty of people beating down his door with advice and opportunity.

'They wanted to see experienced CEOs and CFOs, so I literally signed away my management rights to the company. About three months after I signed everything, the dotcom bust hit. We could no longer go public and I realised all these seasoned executives didn't have a clue how to run my business. Over the next nine months I walked away from everything I'd built with nothing to show for it.'

To blame Steve's mistake solely on listening to others would be wrong; many of these external factors remained out of his and other people's control. But the fact that he built a thriving business for several years on his own, before becoming blinded by the bright lights and promises that other folk offered, is something that continues to eat away at Steve to this day.

'The decision to sign over my management rights was easy at the time,' he said. 'But the reality was far harder.'

This particular sentence stuck out to me, because after building his company from the bottom up, the thought of signing everything over didn't faze him. It wasn't a difficult decision to make, but surely it should have been? This was, after all, his business, his livelihood and his baby. It reminded me of Rachel Elnaugh and how relieved she was when her company finally went under. Both Steve and Rachel spent far too long listening to other people; the promises of wealth seduced them until they forgot why they had set up their business in the first place. And it's at moments like these that the warning bell rings, because the minute you lose control of your vision, dream, and sense, it's a sure sign that bad news is on its way.

For Steve, this involved listening to investment bankers and their promises of Wall Street success, but who's to say you won't become distracted by mentors, clients, staff members, friends, family, or anyone else you deal with throughout your day? It isn't that other people's opinions are dangerous or wrong, but if you find yourself blinded by them, it's time to step back and consider the bigger picture because you may be walking down a path you don't wish to walk at all.

Be it the seduction of money, fame, people, growth, or whatever else dangles before your nose, surrounding yourself with too many people is a recipe for disaster — or as our title suggests, the spoiling of your tasty pad thai.

After all, it's you who has its best interest at heart.

This leads us neatly on to the last section in Stage One: Shock, which reminds us how important it is to keep your eyes on the all-important visionary prize.

INSPIRED BY STORIES FROM: ISLA WILSON, RACHEL ELNAUGH, STEVE OLSHER, LINDSEY RAINWATER, EMERSON SPARTZ

LOST SIGHT OF YOUR VISION? TIME TO TAKE STOCK!

Do you love or hate vision statements? I used to love them, but working for myself changed that. All of a sudden smarmy folk surrounded me, sharing their vision and mission statements, and how their values were so amazing and worthy. I found most of them to be utter nonsense, and a true waste of an entrepreneur's time.

Whichever camp you sit in, please place your biases to one side, because when we talk about vision in this section, it isn't the two hundred word summary you have in mind. Ultimately, your vision is why you set out on this mazy journey in the first place. It's why you decided to leave the security of a monthly wage to live a life of unknowns. It's what success means to you, and the true value of freedom, happiness, and how to live your one life.

It's probably not about money, and it more than likely doesn't involve saving the planet or solving world hunger, either. But you do have a reason for doing what you do, and the moment you lose sight of this you should take stock and consider what the hell you're doing. You already know about the numerous opportunities that come your way at any given moment. You also appreciate fear, and how it tricks you into panicking and questioning what you do. It's a fantastic concoction of entrepreneurial mayhem, and what makes this ride so fun and wonderful. But it also distracts you and tempts you each day, in the same way chocolate does when you attempt to shed a few pounds.

It results in you losing sight of who you are, why you're doing this, and what makes you tick. It may also be the ultimate warning sign because it questions why you'd put yourself through the stress of entrepreneurship if you aren't going to stick to your ultimate plan?

Losing sight of this brought chaos into Judith Wright's world, the owner of Wright Angle Marketing, and one of my local town's leading authorities when it comes to branding, communicating, and generally crafting meaningful messages.

Sitting across the table, I saw the frustration in her eyes as she spoke about starting a new project with a client; one who was at the beginning of their business adventure. Having already built a relationship with them, and seeing the potential on offer, Judith worked hard under the assumption that once investment arrived she'd get paid. It began life as a normal project, but before long required more of her energy, time, and resources. Yet she believed and kept faith and continued to provide more and more, because once the investment arrived, she told herself, all would be fine.

'Because I was there from the beginning,' she said, shaking her head. 'I felt reassured that I'd get paid once the investment came in. So even though the original pot of money ran out, we continued to work and provide as much as we could — ultimately allowing our debt to grow larger and larger. I kept going because I believed the investment was coming and everything would be fine, but it never did. It left a big gap in our accounts for a long time.'

As an entrepreneur yourself, I'm sure you'll appreciate Judith's position because when opportunity calls you listen to it. When a new idea presented itself with plenty of potential and investment on the horizon, why wouldn't she jump on board and provide some work in kind? But along the way she lost sight of the bigger picture, the vision she'd set out to achieve when she started Wright Angle Marketing.

'I've learnt not to get too involved,' she said, summing up her tale. 'My client's baby isn't my baby. They're giving birth to their own ideas, and as much as I want to offer support and encourage them — to an extent I always will do — it's their journey, not mine. That's not to say I don't care, but I've learned to keep my focus on my business, which allows me to distance myself from theirs.'

Judith continued to tell me stories about new projects, and how she still works with certain clients in kind. It's part of opening your arms to opportunity and embracing new ideas, but it's vital you don't lose track of your own vision and focus too much on your clients, or a side project, or anything that distracts you from what you set out to achieve in the first place. It's a common warning sign that a mistake awaits, and whether it leaves a gaping hole in your accounts like it did for Judith, or robs you of time, resources, energy, or growth, the point is it takes you away from your true purpose and vision; why you're doing what you do in the first place. When you lose sight of this it's time to take note and reflect what you're doing because it may be leading you down a road you don't wish to take.

Which brings us to a concept you may have noticed crop up a lot over the last few pages, and a particular word that's appeared again-and-again:

Reflect.

The warning signs we've considered don't offer any answers, nor do they mean a mistake definitely awaits. But what they all have in common is that they give you an opportunity to take a step back and reflect on what you're doing, where you're heading, why you seem to be feel apprehensive.

These warning are exactly that; warning signs. They're a sign that something isn't quite right and that you should take note of where you and what you're doing.

Pretending these signs don't exist, or noticing them and sweeping them under the carpet, often means bad news. It's true, some mistakes and failures come about in an instant and you couldn't possibly plan for them or expect them, but most of the time there are signs that rear their heads long before the moment of shock hits.

If you learn to spot these — and most important of all, take a step back and reflect — you may head off a great deal of pain before it has chance to torture you. Which brings Stage One: Shock to an end, and with it the beginnings of Stage Two: Pain.

Before we move forward and meet a host of new entrepreneurs and their unfortunate pain (as you will soon see, it comes in numerous forms), let's recap what you've just unearthed in the first stage of this book. I'm a firm believer that in order to move forward, you must first appreciate where you are and where you've come from. This is the beginning of your #greatmistake, so let's ensure you start it in style.

INSPIRED BY STORIES FROM: JUDITH WRIGHT, MIKE EILERTSEN, MIKE TILEMAN, RICK TIELMAN, TEA SYLVESTER, RICHARD BURHOUSE, PETER HARRINGTON , PAUL KEMP, MANNISH SETHI

STAGE 1: TASKS & TAKEAWAYS

This book attempts to offer you three things: to entertain, educate, and inspire you, and for this reason we end each stage with a Tasks & Takeaways section.

The following recaps what you've just read, sums up the main learnings, and provides a few actionable tasks you can implement into your world today. You can also download a free version of these workbooks at: successfulmistake.com/takeaways

TOP TEN TAKEAWAYS FROM STAGE 1

1) One of the most common attributes of a business mistake happens when **hiring people**, and although a wrong hire can take place in several forms, they all centre around the notion of hiring anyone, instead of ensuring you hire the right someone for your business.

2) **Decision-making** is a constant throughout the Shock Stage that not only creates a lot of initial mistakes, but has the power to make a small one worse when you panic and make *any* decision, instead of going in search of the right one.

3) Although building your business around your **passion** is ideal, it's important you align this with a real **purpose** that serves an actual audience. Neither passion nor purpose on its own offers enough, and it's balancing these two entities that leads to success.

4) Whilst **fear** remains part of the equation at all times, and

plays a common role in many mistakes and failures, it isn't confidence or competence that you need to defeat it, but rather the courage to take the first step, followed by another and another... Wise words indeed, from Debbie Millman.

5) **Communication** is a common attribute in most mistakes and failures and should never be taken lightly. However, it isn't just how you communicate with your customers, staff, and suppliers, but with your fellow partners, and indeed, with yourself. Good communication helps a strong vision grow, and creates a unified goal that everyone can stride towards.

6) There are times you have zero control over your mistake, and whether such **external factors** are borne out of economical, political, or environmental issues, these mistakes remain your own and will place you into the seven stages regardless. In other words, sometimes you become a victim to circumstance, but this is life, I'm afraid — especially life within business.

7) Although some of your mistakes and failures form out of nowhere and produce real and instant shock, more often than not there are **warning signs** that present themselves long before that dreaded moment hits.

8) One of the most common warning signs is when **tedium and boredom** become part of your everyday life, and you begin to struggle to keep your motivation and determination up.

9) Another common warning sign concerning **communication** presents itself in the form of doing too little (losing yourself within yourself), listening to too many people (cooks spoiling the pad thai), or listening to the wrong folk (those dreaded yes men).

10) Whatever the warning signs may be, they do not provide you with answers, or even determine whether a mistake will or will not occur. They are warning signs and nothing more, and as such all you can do is take some time to **reflect**.

~ () ~

TOP TASKS FROM STAGE 1

1) I encourage you to consider your most important current project, and taking each of the seven attributes into account; Hiring, Growth & Expansion, Decision Making, Passion vs. Purpose, Fear, Communication, and External Factors. Write down all the potential mistakes you can think of that could occur related to your current project/product/business/idea.

2) Based on this list of mistakes (you may have 5, you may have 35), write down the worst-case scenario for each, and the impact this would have on both you (personally) and your business.

3) Again, based on this list of mistakes, consider each of the major warning signs (Tedium, Gut Instinct, On Your

Own, Yes Men, Too Many Cooks, Losing Sight of Your Vision) and write down whether any of these are currently present in your world. Be honest with yourself; don't try and sugar coat it.

4) Finally, for the next week, I encourage you to commit to 10 minutes each day (add it to your calendar), where you reflect on these answers, warning signs and potential mistakes, and make notes about how you feel, what you're worried about, and what steps you can make in the here and now to make sure your mistakes don't ignite.

On their own, these tasks may seem strange, but as you work through this book you'll begin to appreciate how these actionable sections help you implement what you learn straight away. Remember, this book isn't here to simply inspire and entertain you, but also to simultaneously educate you.

To make your life easier, you can download an interactive version of these Tasks & Takeaways, which lets you make notes within the PDF itself (and print it off), as well as watch a video tutorial where I go through each task one by one, and explain how and why they are relevant to you.

Download your worksheet at: successfulmistake.com/takeaways

INTRODUCING OUR CHAPTER PARTNER,
FOLLOW UP

My name is Cormac McCarthy, and I'm the CEO at FollowUp.cc: a company that cares deeply about making people's lives easier. Our product is a powerful Gmail toolset that gives our users — primarily salespeople — the capability to be more efficient in their work. We help people work smarter, not harder.

When Matthew approached us and told us how using FollowUp helped him write his latest book, we were intrigued to learn more. And the moment we discovered the premise of the book, we wanted to support him and be part of this journey, because we appreciate the value in mistakes, and how they often lead to greater ideas.

I've experienced this personally, and we've seen it as a team here at FollowUp.

One of our biggest recent mistakes came shortly after I become CEO, whilst we were still building and re-working parts of the team. At this stage, we didn't have a dedicated marketing person, so a member of the technical product team helped out with this; performing various marketing roles, including certain work on the website.

We never intended for this to last long, but our search for the right marketing person took longer than we hoped, and we didn't know what type of individual we would get until we hired them: Would they be comfortable with all marketing aspects? Would they have a particular skillset? What would their background be in? And so on...

As such, our technical member of the team grew comfortable with their role, so when we did welcome our new marketing person on board, it created certain friction; not between these two members of the team as such, rather knowing where one role ended and where the other began.

As the weeks went by, this caused a degree of pain: for our new marketing person who was still getting used to the company; to our technical member of the team who felt like I'd removed some of their control; to the rest of the team, who were affected by all this; and to me, because it added greater stress and worry to my day, and considering I was still new to the business myself, I continued to settle in, too.

It was a frustrating time, and although it never affected our customers or the product, I knew it soon would if we couldn't figure it out. Plus, I worried we may lose this new marketing person, and be back to square one.

But as I look back on this period now, I appreciate it.

It forced us to create new processes within the business, defining each person's role. We also had more meetings and dedicated time to fixing this issue, which I believe has helped us develop a stronger working culture. Everyone in the team now knows we won't sweep issues like these under the carpet, instead choose to do everything we can to address and fix them.

All of this helped me form a greater understanding of the entire business, too, and each person who works here. As a CEO, I believe this is one of the most vital aspects of my job, and although this period brought pain and stress and had the potential to get out of control, I appreciate the massive value it has brought everyone at FollowUp since.

Through *The Successful Mistake*, Matthew's focusing on a topic most people do not, but everyone must from time to time. It's difficult to appreciate all of this during the moment, because it's hard to look past the pain and the worry. But as Matthew shows throughout this book, the pain does subside and new lessons form in its place.

So, it's over to Matthew to introduce Stage Two: Pain, and continue this journey we're proud to be part of.

STAGE 2: **INTRODUCING MR BEAM, DANIELS & WALKER**

Tim Grahl hit rock bottom once he realised the mountain bike sites he built from scratch would never make money. They would never allow him to live the kind of life he dreamed of, or look after his young family. He felt ashamed and embarrassed, because how the hell did he let this happen?

It began years ago when he and his buddy decided to setup a site that would review mountain bikes and cater for its growing crowd of enthusiasts. 'We didn't have any money to buy the mountain bikes ourselves,' he told me. 'So we figured that we might get a bunch of free stuff if we created a site that reviewed and promoted them.'

An enthusiast himself, Tim oozed passion and provided a genuine need to the mountain bike community, and along the way he developed quite a name for himself. People knew him. He had authority. He brushed shoulders with the riders he admired, but somehow, he could never make it work.

'We got lots of traffic to our various sites, but I couldn't figure out a way to make money. I didn't have much myself, and had young kids and a wife at home. I was the sole provider, so I felt embarrassed by the whole ordeal.'

Despite appearing to grow in authority and success, Tim suffered financial pain because he was unable to make money from an ever-popular business. He felt emotional pain, too, embarrassed by his lack of growth and un-ticked objectives. And he endured personal pain because he had a young family to take care of, but was letting them down. He, no doubt, suffered physical pain too, because how can you get a good night's sleep when you have a mind bombarded by so much stress, so many questions and so many unknowns?

As we move into Stage Two of your #greatmistake, we'll focus on pain and the various types you may suffer along the way. It's always one of the hardest periods of any interview, when the interviewee shares the difficult moments where they slipped into ill health, lost life-changing amounts of money, their grip on family, friends, and their own mental wellbeing.

We'll focus on four types of pain that crop up again and again, but, before you delve deeper, it's important to appreciate that you'll rarely suffer just one single type.

Come on now, did you really think it would be so black and white?

Take Tim, for instance, a guy who touched upon financial, emotional, personal, and physical pain all at once. This is real life, and as an entrepreneur you're so entwined with your business that it's difficult to separate this from pleasure. So, over the coming pages, where we focus on financial, emotional, physical, and personal pain, please appreciate that most mistakes include two, three or even all of the above.

No matter who you are, and how far along your entrepreneurial journey you may be, pain hurts and becomes part of each mistake and failure you suffer through. Certain pain hurts more than others, but pain is pain. However, as Mr Grahl himself said, 'I try and remember, in those moments where everything hurts, that there's more of the story to come; that everyone I respect and look up to have been here in this moment too, and felt this kind of pain.'

Tim's mountain bike sites fell by the wayside, yet this failure also led him on a journey of new opportunity, and taught him the lessons he needed to learn in order to thrive in his new life. Today, he works alongside authors like Dan Pink, Pamela Slim, Guy Kawasaki, and Ramit Sethi, helping them to create and market their books into best-selling successes. It's a far cry from a few mountain bike blogs, but doesn't this prove you have the ability to transform pain into pleasure? Does this not show you how the most painful of failures can soon turn into your greatest idea yet? I sure hope so, but before you do, you must appreciate how this pain forms, how to pull through it, and what to do next.

So, without further ado, let's turn your attention to pain, and how your mistakes don't have to be as painful as you might imagine.

FINANCIAL

It's strange to think that the vast majority of entrepreneurs you look up to have suffered through financial hardship at some stage along their journey. Whether it be it down to not having enough money to begin with, putting everything on the line, or having it before losing it due to the decisions you make, it's difficult to find someone who hasn't lost sleep over money.

It's part of the entrepreneurial lifestyle, I suppose, and whether money drives your motivation or not, it remains an important aspect of your everyday life. It allows you to keep pushing forward, growing, and living your dream. It means you can keep your employees in clothes and help them feed their families. It's a wonderful and horrendous part of life that takes up so much of your focus, so it shouldn't surprise you to hear that out of all the entrepreneurs I've spoken to, most of them have shared some form of financial agony.

We've already met several individuals who are, today, successful and wealthy and in demand, but lost sleep over the money they lost. Steve Olsher lost it all twice before figuring it out, and Jayson Gaignard racked up over a quarter of a million dollars of debt. You've no doubt heard stories from folk you look up to who suffered through such pain. You see it in their eyes as they delve into the past. It hurts, because nobody enjoys putting their livelihood on the line and facing the possibility of bankruptcy and the issues and shame that come with it.

I've seen financial pain come in many forms, but it tends to boil down to one of two categories; personal and business. The thing is, you're an entrepreneur, so what's the difference? Your business is your baby and part of your family, so even if you aren't personally liable it doesn't detract from the pain you feel when it loses a grand, a hundred thousand, or even a million.

Losing sleep over money surely hurts whatever the circumstance, but that isn't to say you can't grow from it nor uncover invaluable insights because of it.

For instance, I once spoke to the COO and co-founder of Freshbooks, Mike McDermott, and although he lost a lot of money with a few key mistakes, it's these that lead him from a good idea to a great one.

Today, Mike leads one of the most popular cloud-based accountancy businesses in the world, but not long ago he invested a lot of money that placed the future of the business on the line.

'We wanted to help our customers learn more about their financial data, so we invested significant sums into a piece of software,' he said, on a call with me during the early days of my interviewing process. 'The problem was that we were still growing and developing, so didn't necessarily need an enterprise-level tool. Over time, we spent around $1.5 million before we eventually killed the project, and as you can imagine, it wasn't an easy decision to make.'

Once you invest a significant amount of money into something, you face the dilemma of when to pull the plug, when to keep going, and when to place more cash on the table. This is what Mike faced as he had to weigh up his options.

'Knowing when to kill the project was the hardest part, because you keep thinking that maybe it'll work sometime soon; just around the corner. If you stop now you'll waste all this money, whereas if you keep going for a little while longer, you think maybe you can turn it around.'

I suppose it's like the gambler who doubles up until they hit a winning hand; sometimes you win and other times you don't. Luckily for Mike, a couple of his team members became rather invested in this software and the data on offer, so were able to replicate what it did in-house. It allowed Freshbooks to move on from this software without too much chaos, but not before they had thrown over a million dollars into it.

'I suppose sometimes you have to learn things for yourself,' said Mike. 'I now apply what we learned to other areas of the business. I don't think that situations like these undermine your confidence; they build it. You appreciate that you survived and gained a lot of useful information you can use to make better decisions moving forward.'

I don't imagine for a second that Mike enjoys thinking about the time he lost $1.5 million. With hindsight, he's able to look back on the situation and appreciate the lessons learned, but at the time he must have lost sleep. He must have worried. He must have sat in long meetings with his co-founders, deciding whether to pull the plug and count their losses, or keep trying for another week, another month, thinking 'let's wait and see what awaits us just around the next corner'.

Whenever you suffer financial pain like this, you're bound to learn a lot about your business: what works, what doesn't, and so on. But the real gem to take from such torture is the true value that money plays in your world and everything you do; whether money motivates you or not, it remains an important aspect of your daily life.

Whilst Mike continued to tell me about the lessons he learned from this period of losing far too much, something struck a chord with me when he said, 'Rather than go with the most expensive and sophisticated solution, we now consider the cheap and cheerful one; always wondering how we can make it work for us.'

This, right here, demonstrates what Mike learned during this period, and the value he now places on money. It isn't about the most expensive or cheapest tool, in the same sense that it isn't about how much or how little you pay that new member of staff. It's about ensuring that everything that you build, and implement into your business, has a purpose, and the actual amount of money doesn't play a fundamental role in this.

It plays a role, of course, because you can only spend what you can afford to spend, but spending money for the sake of spending money, and buying that new tool because everyone else seems to have it isn't the answer, and sometimes you need to suffer through financial hardship before you realise, respect, and appreciate this.

It's not an easy thing to admit to, because little else creates more stress and worry than money. I've seen the pain visible on people's faces as they mentally delve back to hard times and sad times, the type of times that had a significant affect on their health and family and overall wellbeing.

But this hurt also helps you appreciate the true value of money, which in turn teaches you a great deal about the value you place on things like software, tools, and indeed, your ego. Mike learnt that it wasn't the tools that mattered, so much as how he and his team used them. For Mike, it focussed around software, but for you it could be your offices, staff, house, car, or any number of other distractions that so often result in financial pain.

That's not to say all your money problems and worries are avoidable, because the truth is that some mistakes lead to debt and affect your cash flow, and there isn't much you can do to avoid this once the failure kicks into gear. But even if it does, you should revel in the knowledge that it's this pain that will teach you the real lessons about you and your business. It doesn't make suffering through this torture any easier at the time, but appreciate there are lessons to learn, and that successful people often need to hurt financially before they realise what money means to them.

The truth is, financial pain hurts a great deal, and I don't for a second suggest you waste a whole bunch of money just so you can learn this. Whatever role money plays in your business, life, and dreams, and whatever your perceptions of it may be, it's a fundamental part of life, and that isn't changing anytime soon. It's for this reason that I say there is no definitive line between business and personal financial hardship; not for an entrepreneur. These two worlds collide with one another on a daily basis, so money worries in one are sure to bleed into the other.

We start Stage Two: Pain with financial hardship because money plays such a fundamental role in an entrepreneur's life. Whether your money decisions are the cause of your mistakes, or whether the mistakes you make result in monetary discomfort, you will lose sleep from time to time over money and all the chaos that comes with it; simply put, I've yet to meet a business owner (successful or not) who hasn't. And this is fine, because it's the pain you feel here that teaches you so much about what you truly value and desire from this journey, so if you take anything from this chapter right now, have it be this: take a step back and consider the role money plays in your life, and whether you're happy with this. Because you don't need to wait until you waste $1.5 million, like Mike did, before you begin to appreciate the value of a dollar.

You can choose to start today, because the sooner you appreciate what money means to you, the less severe your future financial hardships will be; and this is the name of the game in Stage Two: Pain.

So, is financial pain the greatest pain of all?

Maybe, maybe not.

It causes a lot of stress and worry, of that there is no doubt, but there's another type of pain that affects you a great deal, so let's delve deeper into the subject of emotions, and see if anything else is as painful as lost coins and riches.

INSPIRED BY STORIES FROM: ARNOLD DU TOIT, JAYSON GAIGNARD, BRIANA BORTEN, CAPRICE BOURRET, CHRIS BROGAN, CRAIG WOLFE, DAN MILLER, DANNY INY, DUANE JACKSON, MIKE MCDERMOTT, TONY ABBOTT, MARK SEAMEN, ANDREW HELM, BRIAN GARDNER, CHARLIE KEMP, DAVE HIRSKCHOP, JACOB HILL, TONY ABBOTT, JOANNA DAVIES, SHARON HERMAN

EMOTIONAL

Before I leapt into this land of entrepreneurship, I imagined most business people I'd meet would be ruthless and cold and decisive. I suppose I'd watched too many movies, likening what we do to Gordon Gekko, Jordan Belfort, and Don Vito.

Don't get me wrong, I've met a few tough characters who would probably sell their mother for an extra five percent of market share, but for the most part I find business people are people, which means they do what people tend to do... Feel.

And I know you're not supposed to take it personally, because business is business, but that's easier said than done.

As we've already established, your business is your business so it's fair to assume that you take it personally when you lose money or you fail, and most of those I've spoken to have let their feelings get the better of them from time to time: be it anger, mistrust, hate, regret, pity or sadness. During a period of mistake making, these feelings tend to be rather negative, but suffering emotional pain doesn't make you weak or inept. It simply makes you human.

Do you think Steve Olsher smiled when he realised he'd lost it all? What about Rachel Elnaugh when her business went under? Did Mike McDermott wake up chirping a tune when he put an end to his $1.5 million experiment?

Some folk are more in control of their emotions than others, but I guarantee we all feel during hardship. You take it personally. Your emotions run wild. You suffer fear, sorrow, shame, worry, anger, surprise, and more. And there's a single emotion that sums up your emotional turmoil rather well:

Disappointment.

When you make a mistake that affects you and your business, you're disappointed. You're disappointed in yourself. You're disappointed you didn't see it sooner. You're disappointed in others. You're disappointed because this is your business, your life and, goddam it, you do take it personally.

When Kate Matsaidaira had finished telling me about her startup, Popforms, she whisked me back in time to share stories about her previous existence in the corporate world. Working for giants like Amazon and Microsoft, Kate had eventually dipped her toe into the startup world with brands like Moz and Decide (acquired by eBay). This led her to setup Popforms and focus more on her own projects, but the world she lives in today — centred around helping people and focusing on bigger picture strategies — is a stark contrast to where she began; as a corporate ladder-climbing executive focused on one promotion after the other.

'For years, I followed this particular journey and career path,' she told me. 'Looking back, I never wanted any of it. I think I based my career on what I thought other people wanted me to do,' Kate continued, explaining how she studied computer science before working at Amazon and beginning her ascent up the executive ladder. 'At Amazon, I was running towards this light at the end of the tunnel. I kept thinking if I got another promotion, I'd be more involved in strategy and the running of the business. If I could just make it up another level, I'd achieve it and be happy.'

As a fresh-faced worker often does, Kate reached for a carrot dangling just out of reach, but she never stopped to consider if she actually wanted to reach it. I see entrepreneurs like this all of the time, setting up a business or starting a new project because they think it's what they should do. Well, along this corporate climbing journey Kate thrust herself into, she realised her love for managing people, let alone being a part of the inner workings of a business. This opened up a new world to her, one that brought greater happiness and meaning.

'I began to look at what really mattered to me,' she said. 'This is what lead me to the startup world and working for brands like Moz. A friend asked me, "If you had all the money in the world today, what would you do every day?" I realised I wanted to work on projects I wanted to work on, with people I wanted to work with, and be location independent whilst doing so. When I told my friend all of this he asked, " Why don't you figure out how to make it happen?" So I did, and found entrepreneurs and people working in startups were living this kind of lifestyle.'

Although Kate doesn't regret her time in the corporate world, it's still hard not to regret the mistakes she made herself. The lesson here is that as long as you grow and learn from your mistakes, they become vital aspects of your journey. Disappointment, on the other hand, is far more difficult to overcome, and this is something I'm sure you can relate to. Kate spent years climbing a ladder she never wanted to climb. She based her career around what she thought other people wanted her to do; indeed, what she thought she had to do. If only she'd figured out what she wanted sooner, who knows where she could have been today.

When you make a mistake, you're bound to feel emotional pain to an extent. Maybe anger breaks through, or shame, fear, worry, surprise… It's part of being human. You *feel* because this is your life and your business, so you're sure to take it personally. And it's for this reason that disappointment is the common emotion that ties all of this together. If you're disappointed in yourself, it shows you care. It proves you're passionate and committed and driven, which means it helps you concentrate your efforts on what you would do everyday if you happened to have all the money in the world. In fact it's possible that disappointment may be the strongest emotion of all.

It's fair to say that if you weren't disappointed in your mistakes, it couldn't be that important to you to begin with. Maybe you didn't care about that particular project or client or business. Maybe it directs you away from where you are, and towards a more fulfilling path.

None of this means you won't feel anger or shame or sadness, because mistakes tend to bring out the worst in your emotions, but so long as a level of disappointment exists, you'll be fine. I imagine this sounds strange, because disappointment and everything that comes with it hurts, so why would you want such pain in your world? Well, in the same way that financial hardship helps you to appreciate the value of money, it's disappointment that helps you focus on what matters most to you; whether what you're doing is a need or a simple want.

The fact that Kate felt disappointed after working hard for promotions that she didn't actually want, proved that she desired more from her career than simply going through the motions and picking up a monthly cheque. So, the next time you make a mistake and you're angry, disappointed, and frustrated at yourself, fear not because it's a sign you're passionate about the journey you're on and desire to build something great.

You can't cling to this disappointment and anger and shame, as you'll see in Stage Three: Bargaining, because holding on to these emotions offers little indeed, but feeling them and hurting because of them, simply proves you're human, and that you care about what you're doing. Of course, this doesn't make the pain any less torturous, although it does give you something to focus on and place your faith in. But make sure you let go of it and don't cling on to these emotions for too long.

This brings us to the end of the two types of pain that are so often part of an entrepreneur's mistakes and failures (financial and emotional), although I'm afraid to say this isn't the end of the tale. There are two other sorts of pain that you may find you suffer from. The first centres around your health and wellbeing, which too often become an afterthought to a go-getter like you. But, as you'll soon see, losing your grip on this is a shortcut to making your situation much worse.

INSPIRED BY STORIES FROM: ALEXANDRA FRANZEN, ALEIS GRANT, CARLY WARD, GREG SMUK, JOCY HUNTER, JOHNNY B TRUANT, KATE MATS, LAURA BENSON, LINDSEY RAINWATER, NICK SIMMS, JACOB HILL, KRISTIN THOMPSON, MOE ABDOU, SHARON HERMAN, SHEILA VIERS

PHYSICAL

If emotional pain puts your mind and sanity under strain, then physical pain takes care of the strain on the rest of your body. When you make a mistake, you step up to the plate and work, work, work to right your wrongs. It's an admirable response, but do you think this helps in the long term?

Maybe your mistake is borne from overworking yourself in the first place, hustling and growing at the expense of your health. An entrepreneur often proves their worth and shows how much they want it through hard graft like this, but how long do you expect to keep it up?

Time's apparently relative and gets rather complex in the ether of space, but here on Earth it's simple: you and I have twenty-four hours each day; seven days each week; fifty-two weeks each year.

That's it.

You can't add an extra day after Sunday, or a few hours to the end of each evening (although if you figure out how, please let me know), which means you must use the time you're given wisely.

Neglecting sleep, your health, and diet may seem necessary when starting a business, but is it? Maybe you justify overworking yourself after you make a mistake, but it isn't the answer. A sleep-deprived version of you works slowly, as does an overweight, sluggish, and sick one.

Cramming more work into your day is fine, but all you ultimately achieve is a less efficient and productive member of the team, or even one that eventually falls off the cliff, like Chris Cerrone did in 2014. Founder and host of *The Cerrone Show*, Chris found his podcast go from strength to strength rather quickly.

Before long, he had a bonafide business where people hired him for speaking gigs, coaching, consultations, and sponsorship. It wasn't by accident, because he began his podcast with the aim to succeed, and his attention to detail set him apart from most other shows.

But it's one thing planning for this, and another living through it.

'I was driving along the freeway one evening,' Chris said. 'When all of a sudden I felt drunk and could see tiny black spots in the corners of my eyes. I was on my way to my co-host's house to record an episode, but I had to call her and say, "Laci, we cannot record tonight. There's something wrong. I feel weird."'

Thankfully, Chris returned home in one piece, but this wasn't an isolated incident.

'Over the next few days it got worse,' he said. 'My wife kept saying I had to go to the doctors, so I eventually did. The doctor said I was severely dehydrated and under a lot of stress, which took me by surprise because although I'm not overly healthy, I do okay. I eat well. I'm active. I looked back and wondered what caused this, realising everything I was doing for the podcast, the coaching calls, the course, the speaking engagements... It was all too much. I tried to do it all myself, some days waking up at 4:30am and go, go, going all the way until eleven at night.'

As I spoke to Chris, he worked his through a huge bottle of water. I looked for signs of ill health, but he seemed like an average guy with as much energy as I had. Our conversation came a few months after his trip to the hospital, so in a short space of time he'd regained his health and wellbeing.

'That trip to the hospital opened my eyes,' he said, holding up his big bottle of water. 'One of the worst things was, it affected the quality of the show. I was proud of what we produced, but during this period where I overworked myself, we put out sub-par content.'

The very quality that opened up doors for Chris in the first place, vanished because he overcommitted and overworked. He faced a few tough decisions, like all entrepreneurs face, and it led him to cut ties with clients and outsource a chunk of his work, regaining his grip on what he'd lost, bit by bit.

Ari Meisel was someone else who lost a grip on his health. When I came across Ari one day, I knew him as an in demand speaker, author, and authority figure within the productivity space. His mantra, 'less doing, more living', resonated with me, so when I delved deeper and found that he'd fallen victim to Crohn's disease, and found a way to manage this incurable illness, I needed to hear more of his story.

'When I started in real estate in 2003, I was twenty-three years old. I worked hard and learned a lot, but I still found myself $3 million in debt.' Ari said, connecting the dots between who he is today and who he was back then. 'I worked fourteen hour days on the construction site, smoked a pack of cigarettes each day, ate fast food at least twice daily, and drank each evening with the crew. Overall, I beat the crap out of my body, and it was around this time that I developed my Crohn's disease.'

Ari's lifestyle may or may not have played the defining role in his disease, but it's safe to assume it didn't help, and it's this that forced Ari into making huge lifestyle changes. He began to track everything he ate and drank. He exercised more and changed his diet, analysing everything he did and didn't do. He hacked his system, found new ways to work, outsourced, and spent more time living and less time doing.

After a while, his symptoms dwindled to nothing and he overcame an incurable disease that he firmly believes was caused by his overworking and hustling. He made mistakes and dug himself a hole full of debt, so it's fair to see why he worked, worked, worked. But it wasn't overworking that helped him escape, it was taking charge of his health and lifestyle.

Chris and Ari's mistakes were borne out of overworking themselves, but whether your ill health is the mistake itself or one of the after effects, it's a dangerous and painful place to find yourself in. Whatever the situation, the common end result is a newfound appreciation towards your health and body.

Both Ari and Chris hit an impasse that forced them to take action. As a result, they appreciated everything they did in a whole new light.

Now, I'm not saying you should sit back and relax when you make a mistake or fail, because you have work to do. But overworking yourself to the point where it affects your health is never the answer. You only have one body. You only have one life. There are only twenty-four hours in the day.

An overworked, unhealthy, and beaten body won't help you, whereas a happier, lighter, and faster one works quicker, with greater focus and produces far better ideas.

As Ari said:, 'Because my body was broken, my mind was, too. I was unable to come up with good ideas and make good decisions.'

We've already focused on how important it is to make good decisions, so it's fair to say your health plays an integral role in your journey. As a final caveat, don't forget that physical pain is the one agony with the power to end you; literally.

This is your health, remember. This is your one life. When you fail, you work and hustle; an admirable and understandable solution, but one that rarely produces the correct answer. Taking control of your health, on the other hand, worked wonders for Ari and Chris, and numerous others I've had the pleasure of speaking to. It doesn't just help you, but has the power to invigorate those around you, too. Which brings us to our final port of call in Stage Two: Pain, and the personal hardship that so often comes after a dreaded faux pas.

INSPIRED BY STORIES FROM: ALAN KIPPNER RUE, ARI MEISEL, CHRISTINE RICHMOND, TOM GREVERSON, CHRIS CERRONE , PAIGE ARNOF-FENN

PERSONAL

As a species, we try to segment life into different compartments: business, family, friends, pleasure, and so on...

The thing is, life is life.

You can try and split it into separate chunks, but you may find they overlap one another regardless. This is never more apparent when describing an entrepreneur, because your business is your baby, remember? You can try not to take it personally, but you more than likely will. You can try split your personal life from your business one, but before long they intermingle. You don't have a standard nine-to-five existence, and your life's far from black and white. It's ever-evolving and colourful, which is wonderful, if you ask me, but it does mean that the mistakes you make in one area may affect aspects of living that you wish they didn't.

Business mistakes often lead to personal hardship. Maybe this affects your family, a relationship, or forces you to cancel that well overdue trip. It works the other way around too, of course, because if something goes wrong in your personal world (sickness, divorce, moving house, etc.), it's bound to affect how you work.

You only have one life, so rather than separate it into chunks, maybe you should embrace it as a whole. And we'll look at this notion in a moment, after I've introduced you to a friend of mine, and a story that redefined her purpose.

Stephanie Roper, also known as The Wardrobe Angel, has built quite the following in the fashion and upcycling world. I'm proud to see her continued rise to fame as she features on TV and in magazines, but not long ago she lived with her parents after having her life tipped upside down.

'In 2008, my then partner and I decided to move to Dubai in order to take advantage of the tax-free savings and enjoy a new lifestyle,' she said, standing next to her favourite blue mannequin. 'As soon as we arrived, I felt horrifically homesick and lonely. My partner found friends, enjoyed the lifestyle, and fitted in well. But after six months, the relationship broke down. I was a shadow of my former self.'

Stephanie is one of the bubbliest, most outgoing people I know; she always brings a certain buzz to the room she's in. I imagine she left for her Middle Eastern adventure full of hope and enthusiasm, but we can never be sure how our bodies and minds will adjust.

'He offered to pay for me to return home for a week, but as soon I got on the plane I knew I'd never go back to Dubai. I remember flying into Manchester, as snow covered the hillsides, excited and happy to be home.' She laughed, disturbing her renowned red lipstick. 'But reality soon kicked in, because I had no job, nowhere to live, and no real money to speak of.'

As she waited for her belongings to be shipped back from Dubai, she had to live a rather frugal life, one which helped her see how much stuff she owned, and how she'd built her identity around acquiring things. This led her down a path of helping other people de-clutter their lives, take a new approach to their wardrobe, and sparked the beginning of the thriving business she owns today. Yet this came during a low point in her life, leaving behind someone she loved; the man she spoke to about marriage and children.

Of course, Stephanie's not the only person to suffer in this regard. Someone else who placed strain on his personal life is Ron Holt, the founder of Two Maids & A Mop, one of America's leading cleaning companies. Speaking to Ron before our interview began, I discovered entrepreneurship was his ultimate dream growing up. He wanted to be his own boss. He wanted to own a business. He wanted to create his own version of the American dream, and after years of saving and being a good employee, his big moment arrived.

'The story starts in 2003,' he said. 'We were all set to purchase a maid cleaning service in Florida, although we were based in

Atlanta at the time, so we had to make a big move. I uprooted my family, changed my career, and left my home, all because I dreamt of owning my own business.'

His entrepreneurial tale put a smile on my face, but he soon wiped it off with what he said next.

'We made the move after I did my due diligence, and once we arrived I met the business owner and sat across the table from him. I remember the moment well, especially when he said, "I'm out." We moved from Atlanta. I left a great job. We sold our home, all so we could move to Florida and live the American dream. Only now, there was no business to speak of.'

Ron's mistake came down to a lack of research, I suppose, or not signing and sealing the deal before making the big move. He could have done things differently, but he and his family were excited to start a new life. The American dream, after all, doesn't include a last minute change of heart.

'There were some rough days that followed, but it was a tremendous blessing in disguise,' Ron continued, as he spoke about his newfound motivation and determination.

This pain drove him to new heights, but I imagine the agonies he and his family went through were massive. I'm sure you've heard such risky stories before, when someone places it all on the line, but it wasn't just Ron who found himself affected by this. He wasn't just waving goodbye to some money, he'd moved his family across the country. His kids changed schools. His life, for better or worse, would never be the same.

You can try and separate your business and personal life if you wish, and maybe one day you'll succeed, but life is life. You only have one, so no matter what your mistake is, it's going to bleed over into other areas of your life in some form. It won't always devastate you like it did for Stephanie and Ron. It doesn't always lead to divorce or cross-county moves. But the fact is, your mistakes and failure affect other people; your family, friends, your employees family and friends.

Rather than separating your life, maybe embracing it as a whole is the way to go. This way you involve those who you trust and love, and as we saw in Stage One, involving other people is an important part of transforming your mistakes into success.

Dwelling on this personal pain is sure to send your emotional wellbeing into a spiral, which is bound to affect your health and everything else. Financial, emotional, physical, personal... We may have touched upon them all separately, but they rarely stand alone because pain is pain. It hurts in all forms, and one often leads to another. Sure, they each have their own unique calling cards, and certain mistakes affect one more than the other, but these four agonies tend to overlap and intermingle because entrepreneurs don't live black and white lives; we live in the midst of colour and chaos, which is one of the best parts of owning a business to begin with.

We began Stage Two with Tim Grahl's tale, a mistake that cost him money (financial pain), affected his family (personal pain), caused a few sleepless nights (emotional pain), and dare I say sent him to the fridge or bottle a few times (physical pain).

Pain is pain, so don't worry if you feel it the next time you fail. It hurts and has the power to rock your world, but often helps you appreciate the bigger picture if you give it time. Like Stephanie told me, 'Even though Dubai robbed me of nine months, the reason I started my business — and everything I've built since — is because of it.'

You're not reading this book to regret or hate your mistakes, you're reading it to overcome them, learn from them, and transform them into your best ideas yet.

Fighting through your pain is part of this process, which leads you on to a new stage. Stage Three: Bargaining. It happens to be the most pointless stage of all, not in the sense that you shouldn't read about it, but rather that you shouldn't stay in it for long because there are few lessons to learn.

But before we get to Stage Three and the stories within, let's recap where you've been, what you've learned, and how you can implement this into your world today.

INSPIRED BY STORIES FROM: CLAUD WILLIAMS, ERIN BLASKIE, JEFF BULLAS, MARSHA SHANDUR, RON HOLT, STEPHANIE ROPER, TIM GRAHL, DESIREE EAST, ZOE JACKSON, JARED O'TOOLE, ANDREW COOPER

STAGE 2: TASKS & TAKEAWAYS

As with Stage One, the following recaps what you've just read, sums up the main learnings, and provides a few actionable tasks you can implement into your world today. You can also download a free version of this workbook at: successfulmistake.com/takeaways

TOP TEN TAKEAWAYS FROM STAGE 2

1) Although there are four main types of pain (financial, emotional, physical, and personal), it's rare to suffer only one when you make a mistake or you fail.

2) No matter how wealthy or famous a person may be today, at some point along their journey they have lost sleep due to money and **financial** worry.

3) **Financial** pain is real, and money remains an important part of what you do at all times, but it's often periods of financial hardship that helps you appreciate and value the true meaning of money, and the role it plays within your life.

4) There are a lot of **emotional** feelings that bombard you during Stage Two (most of them negative), but the one that often overrides them all is disappointment.

5) This **emotional** pain, albeit hard, often helps you appreciate what you're doing and how much you care about it, because if you're not disappointed during a

mistake or failure, you need to ask questions about how much you care about the path you're on.

6) If emotional pain tortures your mind, it's **physical** pain that takes care of the rest of your body through exhaustion, disease, and potentially so much more.

7) Although often overlooked during the pursuit of success, it's your **physical** health and wellbeing that determines so much of what you do; your decision-making, energy levels, and mood, to name a few.

8) Although you can try and separate your business and **personal** lives, it's often hard to do so because your business is your baby and means so much to you. Overall, your entrepreneurial journey isn't nearly as black and white, nor as simple as this, and creating a clear line between the two is difficult to do.

9) When you hurt and suffer, those around you *(those you love and treasure the most)* also tend to go through the same pain as you. Although your pain may be **personal**, it doesn't end with you.

10) Above all, pain is pain, and all four types tend to bleed into one another, affect one other, and intensify the torture. It's rare to only suffer through one type at any given time, so prepare yourself for a cocktail of various **pain points.**

~ () ~

TOP TASKS FROM STAGE 2

1) Create a header for each of the pain types; Financial, Emotional, Physical, and Personal, and then list 5 pain points, worries, or negative emotions that you're currently experiencing under each. It doesn't matter how big or small this pain may be, simply be honest with yourself and write whatever comes into your mind.

2) Based on this list of pain points/worries, grade each one out of ten depending on how much they are affecting you right now

    10 = hurts a lot / 1 = a slight worry.

3) Pick your three highest graded pain points, and create a list of possible solutions under each *(ideas that will lessen the pain and make things easier)*. There are no right or wrong answers, simply write whatever comes to mind.

4) Finally, commit to tackling *one* of these solutions/ideas each day for the next week, and at the end, reserve 10 minutes to consider how you now feel about these pain points/worries, and whether you've made a positive impact on your world.

On their own, these tasks may seem strange, but as you work through this book you'll begin to appreciate how these actionable sections help you implement what you learn straight away.

Because remember, this book isn't here to simply inspire and entertain you, but to also educate you at the same time.

And to make your life easier, you can download an interactive version of these Tasks & Takeaways, which lets you make notes within the PDF itself (and print it off), as well as watch a video tutorial where I go through each task one by one, and explain how and why they are relevant to you in the here-and-now.

Download your worksheet at: successfulmistake.com/takeaways

STAGE 3: **IT ISN'T ME, IT'S YOU**

Not long after he'd graduated university, Francis Pedraza had an idea. As a budding entrepreneur with a startup in mind, the world was his oyster, and one day he met someone in an airport who introduced him to Peter Thiel (co-founder of Paypal), who invested in Francis and Everest, kickstarting his adventure into the wonderful unknown.

'I spent an entire year raising $1 million, but felt like shit the entire time,' Francis said. 'The problem was, we burned $100,000 each month, so spent it faster than we could raise it.'

Everest was an alternative to the likes of Facebook and Instagram, that has since closed its doors; it let you document and share your journey and goals online. It struggled, like many startups do, to find its identity and structure, and much like you, Francis worked hard and continued to push the boundaries, hustling and bustling each day.

You know the pain your mistakes put you through, and how they tempt you into overworking and neglecting yourself. Francis kept plugging away and refused to give up, but his whole ordeal taught him a great deal about business, life, and himself.

'I learnt that hard work is often an avoidance strategy; an excuse for not making the hard decisions.'

Overworking himself, and placing too much strain on his team members, Francis tried to fit Everest into a hole it couldn't fit into. He spent money he didn't have to. He focused on metrics that didn't provide the right answers. He pushed and pushed, enticing investors along the way, but their money only placed a bandage over the wound rather than healing it altogether.

'Because of my pride and my ego, I persisted and stayed true to our strategy,' he said. 'I felt guilty I wasn't succeeding, so I tried harder instead of cutting our losses and making hard decisions. If I'd have made some of these earlier — for instance, letting a few people go or changing our overall strategy — I'd have avoided an entire year of pain.'

In Stage Two you tackled pain and its various forms but I'm afraid the hardship isn't over just yet. In Stage Three your attention turns to Bargaining, which is the part of the process that wastes your time more than any other.

If you consider the concept of bargaining, it portrays a feeling of hope. You hope to get a better deal, and, if you bite off more than you chew and receive something you didn't bargain for, you hoped for one thing, but were given another.

When it comes to bargaining and your mistakes, you hope and wish and pretend they don't exist. You blame others. You blame yourself. You embark on a guilt-riddled journey. Maybe you procrastinate and focus on meaningless tasks, or maybe you over-think everything, dwell on the situation, or strive for perfection before moving on.

When I spoke to Francis, he talked about seeing his family around the holidays, and how everything hit him all at once: the long days, the neglected relationships, the stress and guilt of it all.

'I tried to force change through hard work, when I should have been making hard decisions, instead,' he said.

Over the coming pages, we'll focus on procrastination, blame (blaming others and yourself), and the fine balance between over-thinking and over-doing. When you make a mistake it's often easier to pretend it doesn't exist or isn't as bad as you fear. You hope for a better situation, so you blame or procrastinate or over-think. The thing is, all you do is cling to false hope. You try to make yourself feel better, and find a little extra time, but time for what? To take action? To find the perfect answer? To watch as your mistake fixes itself?

You may find Stage Three the most fruitless of all, and one which offers few positives. You learn and grow from shock and pain, but what will you learn from wasting time? Before Francis and myself bid farewell, he shared a nugget of wisdom I won't forget:

'You can't see the big picture and the potential it offers if all you feel is guilt for the mistake you made.'

Bargaining, like hope, locks you in purgatory. It prevents you from moving on and pushing through the other side. You dwell on your mistake instead of overcoming it. But you don't need to bargain with your mistakes, simply learn and move on from them.

I'm happy to say that Francis has since moved on from the mistakes he made with Everest, and continues his entrepreneurial journey with new ideas and business ventures. But he didn't get there before wasting a little time, although he's not the only one, as you'll soon see.

FACING THE MUSIC

Have you ever stayed in a relationship with someone in the hope it would get better? Deep down you know that the two of your aren't right for one another, yet you wait and give it time and hope for the best because you want to make it work, but all that tends to happen is that you delay the inevitable and make things harder for both of you further down the line. You run away. You hide. You refuse to face the music. You've been there yourself, I bet. I have, and not just when it comes to partnerships, but in every other facet of life, too, including business.

You can call it procrastination if you like, but this isn't always the case. Sometimes you genuinely try and fix the issue in hand, you're proactive and productive, and make all the effort in the world. But sometimes you can't fix it, and like Francis Pedraza said, 'Hard work is often an excuse for not making the hard decisions.'

When it comes to your mistakes and failures, it's hard to face the music. Facing the music means you must admit you're wrong or in pain or you've run out of money. It isn't easy, so instead you bargain with yourself and hope for the best. But let me ask you this: How do you think it turns out?

One of my early mentors, Christine Richmond, helped me a great deal during the formation of my Turndog empire. In fact, it was Christine who I talked to about this very book idea, including the title, the structure, and the overall premise and plot. An experienced business consultant, Christine's been there and done it, working on both her own business and with many others. Despite this, she still owns a locker full of mistakes, and one of her biggest rumbled on and on because she refused to face the music.

'The first few months went well,' Christine said, sitting in my kitchen as she told me about one of her first clients; a client that paid well, but didn't provide the type of work she aspired for, 'but then we renegotiated my contract, and they wanted more hours and work from me. The thing is, this came during a time when the rest of my business took off with the type of projects I wanted to work on. But this project got bigger and bigger, and took up more and more of my time, which prevented me from doing the work I wanted to do. As such, it prevented my business from growing.'

Christine knew this client didn't offer the kind of work she wanted from the outset, but as a new business you take on the jobs that come along. The mistake wasn't in working with this client, but rather dedicating too much time to them during a period of continued growth. She hoped it would get better. She assumed she could handle the increased workload, despite it affecting the rest of her business.

'I had a contract with this client for a full year, but began to wonder how I could get out of it. I tried a few times, but to no avail.'

Tiptoeing around the problem and refusing to face the issue head-on, Christine's mistake wouldn't budge, and the pain she suffered grew. She laughed as she told me all this, wondering what took her so long; wondering what stopped her from taking real action sooner.

'In the end, I cut to the chase and got in touch with the owner,' she said. 'Until that point I'd dealt with one of the managers, but decided to go directly above her, despite this being something I wasn't supposed to do.'

Although she was worried about what might happen and that her contract would lock her into this work for several more months, the owner understood and released her from her duty. Christine faced the music, and lo and behold it wasn't nearly as bad as she'd built it up to be.

'Overall, I let it carry on for too long. It took me five months to finally get in touch with the owner and sort the issue out. I was, quite honestly, a coward.'

We may have left Stage Two and pain behind, but you won't escape the hardship until you actually move on. Hoping for the best and hiding from the issue locks you into pain. It prolongs it, intensifies it, and sometimes creates more of it. You can't simply accept you've made a mistake and expect that to be it, because you have to face the music and physically push past it. It's a battle, and just because you own up to it doesn't make it easy. It's a first step, but one of many more to come. Christine didn't push past this first step though, and all she got in return was five months wasted; five whole months she could have grown her business and worked on the projects that she loved.

Whatever your mistake may be, it's often easier to place it to one side and hope for the best. Facing the music is hard because it requires you to stand tall and be brave, but you'll remain in this dreaded stage until you do just that. Plus, as Christine found out for herself, it probably won't be as uncomfortable as you build it up to be in your whirring mind. Once you face the music, and take actual action, you may find yourself leaning back in your office chair and saying, 'You know what, that wasn't so bad.'

Remember, hard work doesn't mean you face the music. This section isn't about procrastination or filling your time with busywork, either. After all, Christine worked her socks off during this period, and did so on a project that paid good money, but this didn't fix her actual problem, and it was this that made her mistake all the more severe. The key to tackling this stage is to face the music, make the hard decisions, own up to your mistakes and literally do something about it. Above all, you need to move on because without doing so, how can you possibly stride onward and upward and transform your mistake into success? I'd argue that you can't, which is why I loathe this stage of bargaining so much.

It doesn't get any better, I'm afraid, because if refusing to face the music doesn't lock you into a state of being a lame duck, what comes next most certainly does... Blame. Ah, the blame game; I'm sure you know it well.

INSPIRED BY STORIES FROM: CHRIS BROGAN, CHRISTINE RICMOND, DEAN PHILLIPS, DUANE JACKSON, JASON GARCIA, MIKE MCDERMOTT, FRANCIS PEDRAZA, AJ LEON, JOHN LEE DUMAS, NAOMI TIMPERLEY, KRISTI HINES, SHARON HERMAN

THE UNNECESSARY BLAME GAME

If there's one thing sure to prevent you from moving on, it's blaming other people — or arguably worse, blaming yourself. You're an entrepreneur with lots to do, and there's a good chance other people will let you down. Whether it's a team member, a supplier, or a big client, there's often a reason to blame someone else.

Of course, you could always play the mature card and refuse to blame others, instead choosing to blame yourself. Really? Does blaming yourself help the situation? Will it help you overcome your mistake and failures? Will it allow you to transform your situation into a success, or will it instead lock you in this woeful purgatory we call bargaining?

I appreciate that other people *are* to blame from time to time, and depending on the situation you may need to fire them, cut them loose from your client base, or search for a new supplier. Maybe you are to blame, too, and you should take a hefty slap on your wrists. I'm not suggesting you remove blame from the table altogether, just that you refuse to dwell upon it.

It may feel good to place blame on to someone else, but it doesn't help you move past your mistake. I once sat in a massive black Range Rover with Caprice Bourret, the famed model and founder of *By Caprice Lingerie*. Sharing her great mistake about how a South African company cost her time and money, she focused on blame and how she refuses to place it on others.

'Make yourself accountable,' she said, her succinct tone shining through. 'Mostly, people blame the whole damn world for their misfortunes and mistakes. No, you are the one who will make your success happen. You! Nobody else.'

A true fighter, with a never quit attitude, Caprice talked about succeeding in the modelling world before humbling herself in the business one. She made mistakes, as we all do, and few were bigger than when she moved her brand into a new culture.

'I struck a deal in South Africa, and let me tell you it was a whole new world. I sold to one of their largest department stores, and literally had over half a million pounds worth of stock on the ocean when they called to say, 'We don't want it all. We only need half. I took a huge beating on this because not only did I have a lot of wasted stock, but I also had to pay taxes on it. Plus, I couldn't get rid of it because it was all in South African sizes, so worthless in places like the UK.'

Shaking her head and reliving the experience, it was clear to see she took this to heart. Sure, she'd made mistakes, could have done things differently, and came away with lots of lessons learnt, but here was a customer doing the dirty on her. She could have blamed them, and for a while she did, but to what avail?

'Don't blame others,' she said. 'Take responsibility for everything, including your mistakes and your rewards.'

Caprice regrouped, took the hit, and moved on from this situation. Blaming the South African customer proved nothing, in the same way that refusing to expand into other countries because of this one failed deal would. She told me about alternative methods, what she does today to avoid such issues, and how this one big mistake lead her to larger sums of money further down the line. But it's her outlook on blame I took with me: 'Don't blame others. Make yourself accountable.'

Notice that she doesn't say blame yourself, either. Make yourself accountable, sure, and take responsibility for your mistakes (*even if they aren't yours*), but don't dwell on it and take the blame. Blaming yourself may be worse than blaming other people; you riddle yourself with guilt and push yourself deeper into the hole you've dug. Take Maneesh Sethi, the founder of Pavlok, and a guy who spent years building a successful blog, *Hack The System*, by partaking in some rather extreme bets.

Today, Pavlok helps everyday people like you and me to overcome bad habits — smoking, drinking, hitting the snooze button — by providing a gadget that gives out a mild zap that trains your brain to stop liking said habit. It looks a little bit bit like a watch, but a watch that electrocutes you. Since its launch, this electrifying device has built a rabid fan base, but it only came to be after Maneesh struggled through bad habits of his own for years; although, on reflection, he realises they weren't necessarily all that bad.

'My biggest failure was not accepting my personality type, and instead trying to live up to society's version of success,' he said, whilst wearing one of Pavlok's early prototypes. 'I began to research different personalities and realised that mine is the type that comes up with ideas, whereas my brother tends to be good at executing them.' His brother, Ramit Sethi (founder of *I Will Teach You How to Be Rich*), is an important piece of this puzzle, considering he's an über-successful entrepreneur in his own right.

Comparing himself to his big brother, and other successful folk, Maneesh gave himself a hard time for losing focus, moving from one project to another, and struggling to become the version of himself he assumed he had to be.

'What I took from this was that I have to accept my personality for what it is,' he said. 'I need to optimise it by surrounding myself with those who let me focus on my strengths and what I do best.'

This is what led Maneesh to bets, challenges and hacking his system in order to find his most effective way of learning, which eventually led to Pavlok and a business that continues to grow. All this came about because he stopped blaming himself, and instead accepted who he was and moved on. In fact, he didn't just move on, he took a stand and built a life around what makes him him. I'm not discouraging you from taking responsibility for your actions, or telling you to assume you're always right, but does blaming yourself for each mistake help you to overcome them? I imagine not, and although Maneesh didn't blame himself for a mistake he made, he gave himself a hard time for being himself. Maybe when you make your next mistake, you'll give yourself a hard time, too. Maybe you'll scold yourself for being so stupid, or for not seeing it coming, or choosing the wrong route. Maybe you'll compare yourself to others and see them overcome mistakes with ease, frustrated that you can't do the same. Blaming yourself prevents you from moving forward, as does blaming other people.

This isn't about letting folk get away with murder, it's about resisting the urge to play the blame game, and instead focusing on what comes next. As I keep stressing, it's about taking action and moving forward, and once Maneesh and Caprice let go of their blame, they soon strode forward and tasted the sweet elixir of success.

Whether it's levelled at you or at others, blame is blame and brings nothing worthwhile to your table. It may make you feel better for a short while, and it may seem like the easier thing to do, but all it does is lock you in this torrid state of bargaining, which as you know, brings few rewards.

Thankfully, we're nearly at the end of it, but before we move on from Bargaining altogether, we need to look at the downsides of taking action, or, should I say, taking action without thinking. As is often the case, there's a fine line to tread, and one that's far too easy to misjudge.

INSPIRED BY STORIES FROM: CAPRICE BOURRET, MANEESH SETHI, JORDAN HARBINGER, DAVE KERPEN, BRIAN FOLEY, ISLA WILSON, NAOMI TIMPERLEY, EMMA AGESE, SHARON HERMAN

THINKING VERSUS DOING

I'm as keen as you are to leave bargaining behind, but before we do, let's turn our attention towards an important crossroads that prevents an entrepreneur like yourself from moving forward to think or to do.

You've just read stories about facing the music, placing blame to one side, and making things happen so you'd be forgiven for thinking that the quicker you move through this bargaining stage and take action, the better. The obvious answer is to *do*, you conclude. Of course that's true, but it comes with a sprinkle of caution to keep you on your toes. Your decision-making skills remain important, and just because you wish to fly through this stage doesn't mean you can do, do, do to your heart's content. If you act without thinking, you run the risk of making matters worse than if you'd refused to face the music or decided to blame others. You need to take action and move forward, but do so with a clear head. In other words, you must master the fine balance between thinking and doing.

When Dave Ursillo started his entrepreneurial path, he didn't quite manage to navigate these criss-crossing roads. An author, speaker, blogger, and yoga teacher, Dave began writing his first book in 2011, full of hope and with a fantastic idea. He thought he was ready so he placed pen to paper, which is fantastic because if there's one piece of advice I've heard more than most on this successful mistake journey, it's to begin, to start, to write... To take that all important first step. But Dave didn't appreciate the entire writing process at this point in time, and as he looks back on his first book, he does so with a certain disdain.

'My biggest business mistake was my first book, which I wrote over a period of eighty four days,' he said. 'The problem was, this book wasn't very good. It had a good message and a solid marketing plan, but because this was my first book, I wasn't sure how to write one.'

Dave's written several books since, so it's not like he's lacking in the pen-scratching department. He chose to do, which is fine, but arguably should have spent more time thinking.

'The book's biggest failure wasn't the mixed reviews, or the fact it didn't result in the success that I'd hoped, but rather that the writing process I'd undertaken didn't honour my values or the message I had to share. I wrote it quickly and by myself, without the help of an editor. I built up a solid readership on my blog, but I didn't involve them.'

Dave took action and refused to stand still, but in doing so not only did he affect the book's success, but also its quality. As you can imagine, this taught him a lot about writing and how to approach future books. He now works with editors. He involves his readers. He takes a more patient and robust process, focusing on quality ahead of velocity.

Patience is an important word during the bargaining stage, because although your instinct is to work through it quickly and all at once, it's important you think carefully about the process throughout. Having read about the dangers of hiding from the issue at hand and blaming others, it's fair to assume you're worried about standing still. Don't be. Be conscious about moving forward and not dwelling on your mistake, sure, but don't be rash. Don't forget to think. Don't forget to take a moment to make sure you're making the right choice.

We've already focused on the dangers of poor decision-making and how this can be the basis of so many of your mistakes and failures in the first place. This still applies, so if you're not careful you can make matters worse — or forge greater mistakes and failures — whilst you try and transform the original one into something better.

Which brings us to back to that all-important concept of hope that defines Stage Three: Bargaining so well. The fact is, once the initial shock and pain of your mistake dies down, you get to choose the path you take. You can pretend the problem doesn't exist or isn't as bad as you fear. You can blame yourself or someone else. You can panic and take action in the here and now, thrusting rational thought to one side. You can even hope for the best by either doing far too much or doing nothing at all. But I'd argue that none of these provides the answer you need to transform failure into success, and each one achieves a single outcome; a prolonged stay in the dreaded stage of bargaining.

I hate to cop out and say something like 'it's a fine balancing act', but it's true. If you want to work through Stage Three with as few issues as possible, you must both do *and* think. Choose only one, and you stay in this interminable stage longer than you have to.

And hope does little help you, either. Remove hope from the equation, because so long as you hope for the best, you run the risk of either doing too much or doing too little, over-thinking everything or ploughing on without a thought in your head. Hope isn't what you need during this period of your 'soon to be' great mistake, but rather the courage in yourself and the decisions you make. Take action, but also remember to take a breath. Move forward and refuse to stay still, but be brave enough to consider each step you take. Place blame to one side (that which you reserve for others, and that which you cling onto for yourself), and focus on what comes after this stage.

As you push through Stage Three of your #greatmistake, you edge ever closer to the tipping point where you turn things around. We're close, but not quite there, because sometimes your mistakes and failures do get the better of you. Sometimes, no matter how hard you try to stay on top, and transform your mistake into success, you slip into a bad place; you hit rock bottom. In some way, we all drift into this torturous state — even during relatively small mistakes and failures, because we're all human, after all. I speak of depression, of course, and although I imagine it isn't something you wish to read about, the fact remains that this stage exists; although possibly not in the way you imagine.

Fear not; it's not the end of the world. Quite the contrary in fact, as many successful entrepreneurs have built their empire on the back of a truly bleak period in their lives. Hopefully you'll never hit rock bottom and suffer the same turmoil as those you read about next, but you'll more than likely slip into depression from time to time, and it most certainly does not make you weak or worthless. You may find this is your most defining period of all, and sparks the moment that ignites your future successes.

But before we get to Stage Four: Depression, let's recap Stage Three and offer a few actionable insights that you can add to your day right now. After all, you don't want to stay in Stage Three for long now, do you?

INSPIRED BY STORIES FROM: DAVE URSILLO, JEN GRESHAM, MARS DORIAN, CESAR ABEID, LISA HAGGIS, DEREK FLANZRAICH, ERIN BLASKIE, JARED O'TOOLE, JEET BANERJEE, JIM HOPKINSON, ELLORY WELLS, OLLIE LEWIS, WILL TROTT, KATE NORTHRUP, KRISTI HINES

STAGE 3: TASKS & TAKEAWAYS

As with the previous stage, the following recaps what you've just read, sums up the main learnings, and provides a few actionable tasks you can implement into your world today. You can also download a free version of this workbook at:
successfulmistake.com/takeaways

TOP TEN TAKEAWAYS FROM STAGE 3

1)   Whilst there are lessons and value to take away from *shock* and *pain*, you get very little indeed from **bargaining**. As such, your main aim is to rush through Stage Three as quickly as possible, and to never look back.

2)   Although refusing to **face the music** often results in procrastinating, this isn't always the case, because busying yourself with lots of work (possibly relevant and worthy work) is often used as an excuse for not making hard decisions.

3)   If you're unhappy or suffering, your issues won't fix themselves by being pushed to one side while you hope for the best. You overcome your hardship by **facing the music** and overcoming it, not by waiting for miraculous intervention

4)   **The unnecessary blame game** comes in two forms: to place blame onto others or to place blame onto yourself.

5)   Although there are times that other people are to blame, and it's indeed they who created your mistake or failure, **blaming them** doesn't solve your issue at hand, or make you feel better in the long term. It simply keeps you locked in Stage Three!

6)   Likewise, there are times that you should **blame yourself** because you're the one to blame, but placing blame on your own shoulders (and clinging to it) doesn't help you to overcome your pain and hardship, nor help you stride onward and upward.

7)   In order to overcome Stage Three, you must **think** carefully and ensure you make the right decisions moving forward, otherwise you run the risk of making matters worse.

8)   But you must also ensure you **do**, because over-thinking and refusing to take action keeps you locked into this stage of bargaining.

9)   As such, the balance between **thinking and doing** is a fine one indeed; focusing too much on one leaves you vulnerable and stuck, which raises the possibility of intensifying your initial hardship, and ensuring you re-live this same pain over and over.

10) Above all, there's a single word that sums up Stage Three: Bargaining rather well... **Hope**. You hope for the best, hope it fixes itself, hope things will get better, and hope for so much more. But it's hope that keeps you in

denial and locked in Stage Three, which is by far the least valuable stage of all.

~ () ~

TOP TASKS FROM STAGE 3

1) Make a list of five tasks that you've been putting off recently (they can be large or small, important or not). You're a busy individual with lots to do, so don't try tell me you don't have five tasks you've been putting off.

2) Over the next two weeks, commit to completing all five of these tasks in full *(let no excuses get in your way)*.

3) Think of a single person you have blamed in the past two years (someone you may hold a grudge against) for something that's gone wrong with your business (a client who didn't pay, suppliers who let you down, etc.).

4) Contact this person and touch base: ask how they're doing, tell them what you're working on, update them on your world, and if appropriate, invite them for a coffee/call.

On their own, these tasks may seem strange, but as you work through this book you'll begin to appreciate how these actionable sections help you implement what you learn straight away.

Because remember, this book isn't here to simply inspire and entertain you, but also to educate you at the same time.

And to make your life easier, you can download an interactive version of these Tasks & Takeaways, which lets you make notes within the PDF itself (*and print it off*), as well as watch a video tutorial where I go through each task one-by-one, and explain how and why they are relevant to you in the here-and-now.

Download your worksheet at: successfulmistake.com/takeaways

STAGE 4: **IS THIS THE END, MY FRIEND?**

You're reading this book in its finished form, but there was a time that I feared you wouldn't read it at all. I found the long ordeal of interviewing 163 entrepreneurs tough, but it wasn't this that placed me on the brink of giving up. Writing these pages didn't come easily, either, nor did the hours of re-listening to the interviews, structuring notes, and staring at the laptop. But again, it wasn't this that pushed me to my limit. Nevertheless, in the early stages of 2015 I did almost give up. Although I had a chunk of the first draft complete, and all those interviews under my belt, I reached a point where I couldn't see light at the end of the tunnel. 'Maybe I'm not good enough to do this,' I said. 'Maybe nobody wants a book that focuses on goddamn mistakes.'

I've made my own mistakes along this journey, not only learning from those inspiring folk I've met, but from myself, too. One of my biggest mistakes occurred in the early days of 2015, after I'd decided to run a campaign for this very book on Publishizer: a crowdfunding platform built by my buddy, Guy Vincent, and one that caters towards the publishing industry.

I planned my campaign and launched it, confidently, sure that

I'd reach my $7,500 target with ease. After all, I'd had over a hundred and fifty authority figures invested in this book, so they were sure to share it with their audience and buy lots of copies, or so I thought.

Predicting this success wasn't my mistake, per se, but rather expecting such help from those who had already helped me so much, many of whom I'd connected with, interviewed, and then left alone; and allowing these new friendships to slip by the wayside.

I continue to regret much of this campaign, but it isn't what I did that's important right now, it's what happened to me next. Needless to say, the campaign failed. I burned a few bridges. I lost money and wasted a lot of time. I went through shock, pain, and bargaining, and unfortunately found myself stuck in Stage Four for a while: Depression. I hit rock bottom and stood on the cusp of giving up.

It wasn't just this failure that came to a head, but other failures and mistakes I'd made, too. All of a sudden I saw them all in front of me, and I couldn't see past the guy I'd become; a guy not good enough, not worthy enough, someone who let fear take over and ruin relationships as a result.

Whether these thoughts were true or not remains irrelevant, because this is how I felt at the time. I slipped into depression and considered giving up not just on writing this book, either, but on being a writer and an entrepreneur all together.

It's a horrible position to find yourself in, but when you make certain mistakes and fail, it happens. So when you read about depression over the coming pages, please try not to associate it with suicidal thoughts, medication, and anxiety. I happen to suffer with anxiety and depression (more on this soon), but that's not to say you'll suffer internally to the point you become ill. This may be depression's definition in society, but not in this book.

In this instance, depression means reaching the point where you can't go any further and you want to give up. Not just on a project or an idea (because sometimes you have to call it quits on a project or idea), but on *you*. That's right, it's about those moments when you stand on the brink of giving up on you; like I did when *The Successful Mistake* Publishizer campaign failed.

It's hard to say how close I was to throwing in the towel, but it certainly felt real. It scared me and shook me up because although deep down I believed in myself and this book, everything else – the shock, the pain, the bargaining – built up and wore me down. I wanted to ease the pain and give up, escape into some corporate office and be like everyone else. I'm afraid to say, sometimes your mistakes and failures will build up and wear you down, too. You may find yourself wanting to pack it all in and escape.

This is what Stage Four: Depression is like, but fear not, there's light at the end of the tunnel — even if it's difficult to glimpse at times. Folk like Dan Miller, Nicole Welch, and Corbett Barr stood on the edge of this cliff, but they found a way through and transformed their mistakes into success regardless. I've met lots of people who wandered into this stage of depression and found their way through the other side, too, not despite the depression, but *because* of it. That's right; this stage has the power to define you! Not in a negative manner, either, but because hitting rock bottom teaches you a lot about yourself. Standing on the cusp of giving up opens your eyes to what truly matters.

When that damn campaign failed, I felt lost and worthless, but it showed me how important this book is. Not just to myself and to those who appear in it, but to the countless people like you who need to read these stories; to learn from them and build a better life on the back of them. I overcame this mistake and low point in my life. I wrote this book. I published it. I shouted about it from the rooftops until you heard me and chose to read these very words. But not before I nearly gave up altogether, because sometimes that pressure cooker cooks you alive and all you wish to do is submit. Just like I did, and fine folk like Jonny B. Truant, too.

THE PRESSURE COOKER

Have you ever woken up defeated, exhausted before the day's had chance to begin? Sometimes one thing leads to another, and no matter what you do, you remain in a slump. You're beaten, tired, on the verge of giving up. I'll wager you've suffered through one or two periods like this in your life, and I know too well how much they hurt.

Such pain isn't exclusively the result of mistakes and failure, but a dreaded faux pas often leads you down such a road. It may start small, but it doesn't take long for it to build, suffocating you in its relentless stronghold whilst it does. It doesn't matter how confident you are, how successful you are, or how beloved you are, either, because although you may seem on top of the world on the surface, it doesn't tell the true tale bombarding you from within. I call this the pressure cooker: that awful time when your mistake builds and builds, slowly wearing you down and abandoning you in the pit of depression. It affects different people in different ways, and just because we call it depression, remember, doesn't mean you're suicidal or turning to the bottle. It just means you're at rock bottom, and on the verge of giving up.

This pressure cooker hurts, but it often leads to your tipping point and your road to discovery, or, as the case may be, a rediscovery of something far grander. I'd like you to remember this as you read the rest of this chapter, and indeed the other chapters during Stage Four: Depression. Enter Johnny B. Truant, who suffered a great deal, but soon picked himself up and regained control of who he was and what lay ahead. You can too, even if you bubble within whilst the pressure cooker simmers away.

Johnny B. Truant is a self-published author these days (including titles like *Write. Publish. Repeat.* and *Fiction Unboxed*), and he's quite the authority figure when it comes to writing, self-publishing, and book marketing. Back in 2007, he focused his time on freelance writing and website development, and, in a bid to add some passive income to his bank account, he turned to real estate. You can imagine what happened next, considering this occurred during a period when the industry imploded.

'We had properties we needed to refinance but couldn't,' he said, describing the time his pressure cooker bubbled away. 'We lost all of the properties to foreclosure, although these were actually a relief, because while we tried to keep them afloat, we were dumping around $2,000 each month. The money came from our credit cards and home equity line. It sucked. It was totally miserable. We couldn't sleep. Because things were so desperate, I was willing to try anything and everything — other than, in retrospect, getting a job. I guess I'm just wired as an entrepreneur; getting a job honestly never occurred to me — so I started researching ways to build a business online. I worked insane hours because I had to, but this was the start of the business that grew into what I have today.'

A man with responsibility, Johnny faced huge turmoil, as well as commitments to his freelance clients. It's difficult to see the light at the end of the tunnel when everything around you crumbles to pieces, and although this period led to sleepless nights and endless worry, it didn't end him. On the contrary, it helped him rediscover his true value to the world, and what he could offer better than any other.

'It took some time and a lot of hard work, but things improved reasonably quickly because I was so single-mindedly focused on how it had to work. The "mistake" of getting myself into real estate drove this change. I wouldn't have had the drive I required to build my online business if things hadn't been as incredibly terrible as they were. I made it work because there was no other option.'

Sometimes your mistake places you on the brink, and as you cling to the edge you're bound to consider giving up. Johnny refused to, as I imagine you'd refuse to do, too. Still, it didn't stop the worry or endless tossing and turning at night, but what it did do was motivate him, focus his attention, and slowly but surely bring him back to the surface. Most important of all, it taught him a great deal about what mattered to him.

'In the end, I learned several things:

1) My interest in real estate had been motivated by greed. I had dreams of getting rich fast, but I've learned this is crap. Real success takes work, not magic systems.

2) My success has to come from my own work. Everything I've tried that has been about magic buttons or arbitrage (like real estate) fails. Whereas everything that comes from me creating awesome, honest, great work succeeds over time.'

In the same way that your emotional, physical, financial, and personal pain from Stage Two helps you appreciate what matters, hitting rock bottom does, too. The pressure cooker builds up to the point where you either give up or focus on what matters to you. Giving up wasn't an option for Mr Truant, so he buckled down, focused on his work, and figured out how he could best serve his audience. It led to his true calling, some might say, which brings me to our next entrepreneurial fellow, who goes by the name Tom Ewer. Founder of Leaving Work Behind, Tom left his job in 2012 to achieve his dream of working for himself. Diving into the type of books you may have read yourself, he decided to place his eggs in the niche site basket: those small sites designed to create links and score well on Google.

'I gave niche sites a go in early 2012, and to say it didn't work would be quite the understatement.' Tom said, around eighteen months after this experiment began. 'I quit my job around this time and poured $1,000 into these sites, but barely made anything in return.'

An approach that's hardly uncommon, Tom used a system that worked for others and attempted to scale from the get-go. But he never gained traction, and whilst his niche sites earned mere pennies here and there, he wrote about his experiences, frustrations, and daily lessons on his blog.

'It was sort of accidental, and to be honest, came naturally to me. I blogged about my experiences with these niche sites because it was a form of accountability; they were therapeutic, in a way. Because of this, my audience literally told me what to write, based on the emails they sent me and the questions they asked. It soon became clear what they wanted from me, and suddenly I had an audience telling me what to do and what to create next.'

Tom's pressure cooker was different to Johnny's, but remember that depression — in this case — doesn't mean you struggle to get out of bed in the morning, it means you reach an impasse and don't know where to turn. And difficult periods like these often offer great clarity. In Tom's case, he wrote about these experiences and shared it with those who needed to read his words. This opened his eyes, helped him focus on his passion, and introduce him to a business he wouldn't otherwise have known. Your pressure cooker may build and place you on the brink, and it may differ to, and affect you differently to me or Johnny or Tom, but even if you're unable to escape your mistake at first, appreciate that this isn't where it ends. You face the choice of giving up or diving deeper, and being the entrepreneur you are, I expect you'll take the latter.

So, how do you climb out of the pressure cooker? How do you escape this darn depression? It often involves asking 'bigger picture' questions, the type of questions you may not have asked yourself before, or at least not had an honest answer to give. For Tom and Jonny, such questions led to a more important road; a path that encourages you to think about who you are and what matters to you the most. So, if you've found yourself in doubt, it may be time to ask a few big and important questions.

INSPIRED BY STORIES FROM: JOHNNY B TRUANT, SCOTT OLDFORD, TOM EWER, STEPHANIE ROPER, JEFF BULLAS, JOEY COLEMAN

WHEN IN DOUBT, ASK BIG QUESTIONS

As a man who suffers from anxiety and the occasional bout of depression, I appreciate how difficult it is to pick yourself up when you're punched hard in the chest. I literally struggle to breathe at times, and whether this is the result of a mistake, business, or life in general, these worries sometimes send me into a spiral.

I remember one of these difficult afternoons, which began in otherwise normal circumstances. One bad day led into another, which led to this unfortunate afternoon where the wrong person said the wrong thing at the wrong time, and everything within my body bubbled and spluttered. Heavy breathing followed clenched fists. My eyes ached in the blinding sunlight. I couldn't look at anyone, but as I walked down the street it felt like everyone stared at me. I wanted to hide and runaway, not just from writing and my business, but from everything; from life; from existence.

I began describing this stage of depression by stating that it doesn't have to involve suicidal thoughts to hit you hard. Depression, in this case, means hitting rock bottom where you're on the verge of giving up; on your business, your dream, your freedom… You. But maybe it affects you more than that, and maybe you've suffered through horrendous moments of panic, anxiety, and emptiness like I have. These periods hurt, and whether they last for minutes, hours or days, you drown beneath your own sorrow and fear.

On this occasion, my panic consumed me for the rest of the day, and after sleeping and bundling my head under the covers, I slowly found my way back to the surface. I still hurt. I continued to ache. I felt hopeless and useless, and that I had nothing of value to offer this world. But before long, I thought about the bigger picture and how this moment wouldn't define me. I thought about my son, and how he will always be the most important part of me. I thought about my family and better half, and how lucky I was to have them. I thought about all my other loved ones, and how I'm never alone. I thought about my health, the fact that I live a life of freedom, and although I have much to do in order to become the man I want to be, I have the power to take control and take matters like these into my own hands.

In other words, this depression put my life into perspective, and over the coming days I not only escaped my low point, but appreciated who I am, what I have to offer, and how I can connect this with those that I need to serve.

I wouldn't, however, recommend searching for a low point in the expectation that it will help you discover your purpose. Nonetheless, these periods in life — however they affect you, and however they come about — offer a greater perspective so long as you ask yourself those all important 'bigger picture' questions.

A woman I admire a great deal reached this dreaded point once, during her trip to Honduras where she set up a not for profit business and worked with the region's gang members. A university professor, and host of the *Real Time, Real Men Only* podcast, Nicole Welch escaped her comfort zone during this period of her life, and although humbling and life changing, it placed a lot of pressure on her and her husband's shoulders.

'What I learned in Honduras changed me forever,' she said, sharing tales about death threats, potential kidnappings, and the various other daily dangers she faced.

Placing the cultural differences of language and etiquette to one side, Nicole had to adapt to a completely new way of living, thousands of miles from her friends and family. It's easy to imagine her hardship and loneliness, and the no doubt difficult nights where she questioned her motive for being there in the first place.

'There were days when I said to myself, "My life's in danger, I'm twenty pounds underweight, and far away from my family… Why am I doing this again?" I remember looking at my husband once and thinking, "I don't like you anymore. Can you take me home now?"'

Although she smiled and laughed as she told me this, I could see the pain she continues to hold. After all, she moved there to help those who needed it, spent her days building houses and offering counsel, and devoted herself to a truly selfless act. In return, she faced daily fears and worrying unknowns. Yet, these low points taught her about herself, and forced her to ask those 'bigger picture' questions. She summed it up well when she said, 'When the going gets tough, you have to know your "why", and know who you are. It's this that keeps you going.'

Linsi Brownson, the owner of Spark Collaborative, a California-based branding agency, faced an impasse like this; although under rather different circumstances. During her business' first iteration, she did everything by the book, followed the rules, and went to all the events she was 'supposed' to.

'After nine months, I burnt out,' she said, describing her frustrating start to entrepreneurship. 'I loved interior design and working for myself, but I began to resent it. There was a particularly bad client that put me in this situation, where I realised if this was it, I didn't want it anymore. But I looked around me and saw other people enjoying their journey, so I knew there was an answer; I just had to find it and figure it out.'

Like Nicole, Linsi found herself close to giving up. Mistakes and failure often lead to feeling like this, because it's hard to see a way out. You begin to believe you're not good enough, or wonder whether this life is meant for you, and think that maybe you'll always struggle and barely keep your head above water.

'I escaped this low point by sitting down and asking myself, "What do I really want?" I sat there and thought, which lead to more questions; "Why did I choose this path I'm on? What do I need to do to get to the next level? What life do I wish to live?" The answers to these helped me identify my core values and define my own set of rules. I stopped following other people's, and instead defined what success meant to me, and what I needed to do to achieve this.'

Linsi's low point helped her appreciate who she is, what she's doing, and how she needs to go about finding her version of success. This dreaded period put her life into perspective, like it did for Nicole.

You're not weak for slipping into depression and nearly giving up. Just because you consider a life outside of entrepreneurship doesn't mean you aren't cut out for it. Such moments never feel good, no matter how they come about, but they often force you to consider the bigger picture and ask yourself those all important questions. As Linsi says, 'Don't be afraid of what the answer may be. It might not be what you expect, or even what you want to hear, but if you're honest with yourself, it will be the right answer.'

When the pressure cooker gets to you and you reach the point of giving up, it's a difficult place to escape from. Whether you suffer with anxiety or not, it's sure to affect you in a big way; a way that feels inescapable at times. But these moments don't have to be the end of you, your business, or your dreams, so long as you ask yourself a few big questions — and, of course, are honest with yourself. And although looking within yourself helps, you shouldn't forget about those around you. That's what we focus on next, and the importance of relationships when everything else around you suffers. It's not about doing this or getting through it on your own, it's about involving those who have the power to guide you along your way.

INSPIRED BY STORIES FROM: NICOLE WELCH, JAYSON GAIGNARD, RACHEL ELNAUGH, IM GRAHL, LINSI BROWNSON, FRANCIS PEDRAZA, LIAM PATERSON, KRISTY OUSTALET, JOCY HUNTER, JAMES CLEAR

THE IMPORTANCE OF RELATIONSHIPS

The depression stage can quickly become a lonely place, and although there's a lot to take from looking within, it's dangerous to tackle it all on your lonesome. We touched upon the perils of going it alone in Stage One, and in the same way it helped Fraser Doherty and John Corcoran appreciate the value of others, hitting rock bottom helps you to see how valuable your friends, family, and overall network are. After all, they say it isn't what you know, rather who you know. I find this doesn't only apply to business, but life in general. And I don't mean it in some seedy manner where your sole aim is to like people in order to ask for something in the future. That isn't a relationship or friendship, it's a manipulation with an agenda at the forefront, so get those thoughts out of your mind.

As you may have realised so far in Stage Four, this period of depression hurts. It pushes you to the brink of giving up, and you lose sight of who you are and what's important to you.

One story I consider, often to this day, came from the lips of Dan Miller; owner of 48 Days, and a bestselling author, podcaster, and true inspiration to thousands. He's been there, done it, and written about it, he continues to touch the lives of others through his calming, inspiring, and motivating aura. When he agreed to be part of this book, I was delighted because this was a guy I'd wanted to meet for a while.

When I jumped on Skype with him, I was nervous indeed, but he soon calmed these nerves by treating me like an equal. Dan's a man at the top of his game, so it always means a lot when such an individual approaches an interview in this manner, although as soon as he began to share his story, I realised why he did.

'I lost my house, cars, everything...' Dan said, describing the aftermath of his failure, and a period of life when he lost it all. 'Although thankfully, I managed not to file for bankruptcy, because I wanted to repay my debts to those I owed.'

This last point is important, but before we get to that, you may like to discover how Dan found himself in this hole. After a successful foray into entrepreneurship, he took his eye off the ball and bought a health and fitness business despite having no interest in the industry. He liked the look of the bottom line, so why not?

This is where his mistake began, but it soon rumbled out of control at a worrying pace when his bank changed ownership. The good relationships he'd built disappeared out of the window, and after making a few changes to his business model, everything came to a head.

'The combination of my cash flow drying up and the bank getting nervous placed me in an untenable position,' he said. 'I ended up selling the business at auction, and when all was said and done, I owed $430,000 and had zero assets to my name. Oh, and part of this debt was to the IRS, so you can imagine this made my situation worse.'

I was shocked. I couldn't imagine how he'd escaped this low point, let alone built his 48 Days empire and crafted such an inspiring journey. It didn't make sense, until he talked about the lessons he learned, and his appreciation for those around him.

'I was embarrassed and humiliated, and was also the chairman for a local chamber of commerce. The morning after this happened, I offered my resignation, because I figured "who was I to help other businesses?" Instead of accepting they said, "No. Now you're really the guy we want. Before, when you were successful, you didn't have a good overview of what most people go through. But now, you're the exact person to help our members." This amazed me and was very reaffirming, because instead of pushing me further out into the cold, they invited me in and asked for my help.'

Being honest with people and refusing to bottle it all up showed Dan that those around him cared. They wanted to help him. After all, he'd spent years building meaningful relationships and being a good guy, and instead of taking bankruptcy when it would have been the easier path to take, he refused to do this so he could honour his debt with those he owed money to. He had to be honest with them and tell them it wouldn't be easy, but they understood. They supported him. They stood by him, like he had stood by them all those years.

'Having that unconditional support played a major role in rebuilding our lives,' he said. 'Plus, I've been married to the most wonderful woman for a long time, and her unwavering support throughout helped me no end. She could have pointed the finger and said a lot of things, but she didn't. She loved me and supported me, that's it.'

It's understandable to feel shame and guilt during a time like this, and more so to keep everything to yourself. Some mistakes literally shake the foundations beneath you, but as Dan shows, it's those around you that help you rebuild.

Despite owing hundreds of thousands of dollars, and letting lots of people down, he allowed other people in, was honest with them, and they repaid him with their faith and support. What more do you need? What greater motivation is there than knowing those around you have your back? Whether it's a loving partner, a lifelong friend, a family member, a recent acquaintance, a customer, supplier, or staff member… It's those around you that have the power to help you back on your feet, whereas the alternative isn't pretty.

'I have a friend who's currently at rock bottom,' Dan told me. 'Over the years, he's sabotaged his integrity and relationships, and right now he has nothing. He's even struggling to find a place to sleep, but I never had this problem. Even at my lowest point, lots of people offered a helping hand.'

No matter what your mistake or failure is, and however low you feel, those around you will help you back to your feet so long as you treat them well in the first place, and prove your worth as a friend. And if you look at yourself right now and don't consider yourself to be a good friend or colleague or peer, what are you waiting for? Don't wait for your mistake to arrive before you appreciate the value other people play. It's what you do today that defines so much of tomorrow, and the sooner you appreciate, value and respect your relationships, the better.

My personal story from the beginning of Stage Four should offer all the proof you need, that if you treat people poorly right now — you take them for granted, do nothing but ask, set expectations and assumptions — tomorrow's mistakes become all the more severe. That isn't to say you shouldn't look within and ask yourself those all-important questions, because you need to do this in order to learn and grow. But doing this doesn't mean you have to tackle this period on your own. It isn't an either/or situation, so place your ego and embarrassment to one side; ask for help; don't push support away or insist you're okay on your own.

But what if you can't quite escape this stage of depression, despite those around you having your back? Well, sometimes you have to flee, but maybe not in the way you imagine.

INSPIRED BY STORIES FROM: DAN MILLER, ALAN KIPPING-RUANE, THOMAS FRANK, NICK UNSWORTH, TABITHA NAYLOR, MARSHA SHANDUR, DAVE KERPEN, DORIE CLARK, JAMES CLEAR, JOEY COLEMAN

TO FIGHT OR FLEE

I imagine you're keen to end Stage Four, because who wants to dwell on something as depressing as depression? Not me, and not you, I'm sure.

However, there's one final piece of Stage Four's puzzle, because even though you battle through the pressure cooker, ask those big important questions, and let those around you share the burden, you may remain trapped. Does this mean you should give up? Maybe. After all, some businesses end. Some ideas are destined for the scrapheap. Not everyone is cut out for entrepreneurship, but just because you make a few mistakes and fail doesn't mean that's you. As Dan Miller himself said, 'I don't think anyone finds success without stubbing their toe a few times along the way.'

Because you're reading this book, I'm assuming that quitting isn't an option for you. That's not to say that you won't have to pivot or put an end to a particular project, but you the entrepreneur, you the go-getter who refuses to accept a life of shackles, are ready to fight the good fight. So, does that mean you can never flee? Is fleeing the situation out of the equation altogether? Is this itself the true measure of failure? Not exactly, because sometimes you need to take a break and escape in order to hop out of the pressure cooker, discover the answers to those all-important questions, and gain clarity when other people offer their support.

Fleeing isn't the ideal solution, but sometimes it's the necessary one.

Because, as the tattoo on my forearm says, 'This is goodnight, not goodbye.'

One man who bid goodnight to entrepreneurship but refused to say goodbye was Corbett Barr: the co-founder of Fizzle, and an online authority figure who's inspired countless bloggers, podcasters, and marketers. Although he's an online champion today, a few years ago Corbett founded a Silicon Valley software startup, and despite having millions in venture capital behind it, it failed and slipped into tech oblivion. The obvious choice thereafter was to get a job, or jump straight back into the entrepreneurial pit, but Corbett decided to take a different route.

'To be honest, it was time to take a step back to revaluate what I wanted to do with my life,' he said. 'So, I took a six month sabbatical with my wife where we decided to take a road trip around Mexico.'

My heart fluttered as he said this, because, for me, the thought of taking a vacation after your business goes under was unfathomable. Surely this was running away from the situation. It was giving up. It was pretending there wasn't a problem. It was all kinds of bad, and the type of thing that we've discussed during the first three stages, right?

Well, no. Corbett wasn't saying goodbye, nor did he pretend a problem didn't exist. It was a chance to disconnect and recharge, and, as he says, 'It was a trip of self-discovery and picturing what my next business would look like. I was in a dark period for a few months, and I knew I wasn't in the right mind to make a serious decision in the here and now.'

In the same way that you have to sometimes step back when you make your mistake (to breathe and evaluate), at some stage you may reach an impasse, and although you ask those big questions and let other people share your burden, it isn't enough. You can't escape. You're too stressed or worried or connected to everything. Sometimes you have to flee, because not only does it lead to a fresh perspective, but a completely new one altogether.

'When we first took this trip,' Corbett said, 'I figured I'd take a few months off to recharge my batteries, and eventually come up with my next idea. I also figured I'd build my next business in the same way as before, gathering investment, but as we travelled deeper into Mexico, we met people living completely different lives to the ones we thought were possible. They weren't necessarily rich, but they'd discovered a model that let them travel and live abroad for many months at a time. I honestly didn't know this was possible, yet here were these people building careers around their lives, rather than existing around their work.'

As he studied what these people did, Corbett blogged about it and took his skillset online, bit by bit, edging deeper into the world he knows well today. If he'd stayed and hustled, started a new business, or found a job –you know, the sensible thing to do; the thing most people would do– maybe he wouldn't have discovered this lifestyle. Maybe he wouldn't be the man he is today..

This entire stage of depression is a giant impasse of sorts, I suppose. It leads to Stage Five: The Tipping Point, where you begin to transform your mistake into something wonderful, and although I hate to use a cliché like 'the darkest hour is just before the dawn', it's true. Depression hurts. The pressure cooker is agonising. You may want to give up, and you may go through hardships you've never been through before. It's part of the entrepreneurial journey, I'm afraid, and when it comes to mistakes and failure, we must all stub our toes a few times.

Confiding in those around you helps, as does searching within and figuring out who you are and what it is you want from your life. Sometimes this requires you to stay and fight, but sometimes you need to flee to figure out the right answers. Corbett did, and in my opinion it makes him one of the bravest people I've met along this successful mistake adventure. After all, there's nothing wrong with fleeing so long as it's to say goodnight, instead of goodbye.

In this instance I wouldn't call what Corbett did fleeing at all; instead it's running towards something, going in search of that all important right answer, rather than settling for the easy or obvious one. The fact is, that your mistakes and failures may build up from time to time, and you may find yourself on the brink of giving up. If you do, maybe it marks the beginning of your time to stand tall and fight, because although you may feel like quitting, it doesn't mean that's what you should do; it doesn't mean you're weak. It simply means your hurting, but it's periods like these that teach you a great deal about yourself, what you want from this, and how you can go about achieving it.

As I hinted earlier, it's often this hopeless stage that leads you towards an ah-ha moment of sorts, which brings us nicely to Stage Five: The Tipping Point. It's here where that glimmer of light sparks your transformation into life, and it's during this stage of the book that you get see how those you admire turned their misfortunes around. This is, after all, why you chose to read this book in the first place. You want to learn how to transform your hard times into your best yet. But the truth is, that these first four stages are tough, full of low points and hard points and painful points.

Thankfully, it picks up from here on in, and that light at the end of the tunnel shines brighter and brighter. It's here you turn your hardships into successes, so before we move on to Stage Five: The Tipping Point, give yourself a hearty high five because you've worked through the tough bits. It's cause for celebration, but before we break out the party hats, let's recap what you've covered during Stage Four: Depression, and how to move forth in the best possible manner.

INSPIRED BY STORIES FROM: CORBETT BARR, DESIREE EAST, JEET BANERJEE, COLIN WRIGHT

STAGE 4: TASKS & TAKEAWAYS

The following recaps what you've just read, sums up the main learnings, and provides a few actionable tasks you can implement into your world today. You can also download a free version of this workbook at: successfulmistake.com/takeaways

TOP TEN TAKEAWAYS FROM STAGE 4

1) Although **depression** can result in medication and suicidal thoughts, in the case of this book, it means reaching an impasse of sorts, and truly considering giving up — not just on your business, but on you and your dreams.

2) **The pressure cooker** refers to the period when your mistake(s) build and build, wear you down, and place you in the pit of depression; a stage where you cannot see the light at the end of the tunnel.

3) Although this **pressure cooker** scenario hurts and makes you question whether you can do 'this', it's during this stage that you must look to the bigger picture and focus on the real reasons why you are, in fact, doing 'this'.

4) It's during tough periods like these that **asking those bigger picture questions** means the most, and because you're vulnerable and weak at this stage, the answers you discover often tell you a great deal about yourself, what drives you, who you wish to serve, and so much more about you and your business.

5) You may also find that the **bigger picture questions** present answers you do not expect, or desire, but this is fine because so long as you're honest with yourself, it's these answers that lead you down the right path, moving forward.

6) Although your gut reaction may be to keep your depression to yourself and not to involve other people, it's your **relationships** that play the most important role during Stage Four.

7) Treating your **relationships** well today (with generosity, giving, helpfulness, caring etc.) ensures that they are there for you when you need them the most tomorrow — not necessarily financially, but emotionally and in a supportive sense that picks you up off the floor.

8) Sometimes you must **flee** in order to escape your depression — not by running away, but by going in search of the right answer, instead of settling for the easiest or quickest.

9) Or as the tattoo on my forearm says, *'This is goodnight, not goodbye.'*

10) Although you may consider quitting the life of an entrepreneur, this doesn't make you weak, nor does it mean you will quit. It simply means you're hurting and suffering. It's this stage of **depression** that leads you to

the light, for the darkest hour is just before the dawn.

~ () ~

TOP TASKS FROM STAGE 4

1) Imagine I've just given you $1 billion this afternoon, and that you now face the prospect of never having to earn money for the rest of your life.

2) Spend thirty minutes making a list of all the things you would like to do with your time, *with the worry and pressure of having to make money removed from the situation*. This list can involve people, projects, locations, items, products or ideas. There is no right or wrong answer, so simply write what comes into your mind.

3) Based on this list, write a 250 word summary of what your average day would look like if you had all the money in the world, and nothing but time and value to share with your audience.

4) Once you have written this, read it and spend ten minutes thinking about it. Consider whether you're on the right track to achieving your goal, and if not, what you can do to start righting your course today — come up with three ideas you can implement today.

On their own, these tasks may seem strange, but as you work through this book you'll begin to appreciate how these actionable sections help you implement what you learn straight away.

Because remember, this book isn't here to simply inspire and entertain you, but also <u>educate</u> you at the same time.

And to make your life easier, you can download an interactive version of these Tasks & Takeaways, which lets you make notes within the PDF itself (and print it off), as well as watch a video tutorial where I go through each task one by one, and explain how and why they are relevant to you in the here-and-now.

Download your worksheet at: <u>successfulmistake.com/takeaways</u>

INTRODUCING OUR CHAPTER PARTNER,
CONTACTUALLY

My name is Zvi Band, and I'm the co-founder and CEO of Contactually, a relationship marketing platform (putting the 'R' back into CRM), whose greater mission is to help professionals build and maintain personal and authentic relationships with their clients and partners.

As I write this, our fifth birthday is coming up, but in the early days, reaching this milestone seemed unfathomable.

Let me explain why and how our **tipping point** came in to play.

Raising capital is one of the most daunting challenges a startup faces, especially at an early stage, because there's so much internal uncertainty: will my idea pan out, who is going to help me with this, what does the product look like?

And on top of this, I faced having to raise outside capital as a young, relatively unproven entrepreneur — necessary capital in order for the founders to make ends meet, hire an initial team, and start to get the product into market.

Investors typically want to invest in one or a combination of three things: the track (there's a big market), the horse (the company), or the jockey (the team). We had none of these, and it was showing because we were getting no, after no, after no.

As much as one shouldn't take these personally, each 'no' felt like a personal rejection, and soon desperation kicked in.

But then we noticed a change, and this is when our **tipping point** came to be; shortly after our first yes.

Beyond the actual capital, the message that came along with it resonated with me deeply, as it read, "I don't know much about what you are doing, but I believe in you and think you'll figure it out."

He was betting on the jockey (me), and I all of a sudden realised that this was possible, and that I would be able to raise the necessary capital to grow Contactually, and that I didn't have to have a clear idea of what the next ten years would bring for us, because all I needed to show was the strength and willpower of our nascent team.

Come hell or high water, we were going to be the team that got something done.

We got that round closed quickly, and with momentum now on our side, we closed the next one; and the next one; and the next one. To date, Contactually has raised over ten million dollars in capital, built the team to 70+ people, and, most importantly, achieved our mission for many thousands of customers.

These days, things are more established, and investors can clearly see our market opportunity and bet on the track, and see the success of our execution to date and bet on the horse. But at the end of the day, what they are investing in remains the jockey; the team and company culture we've created that will power us to achieve our massive vision.

That's one area, despite any ups or downs, I have learned to never stop investing in. And it was this **tipping point** that allowed us to get to where we are today, and continues to push us towards new and exciting opportunities tomorrow. With this in mind, I'll pass things over to Matthew, and Stage Five: The Tipping Point.

STAGE 5: **WAKING UP ON THE RIGHT SIDE OF THE BED?**

There was a time when Michael O'Neal was a true success story, working for prestigious agencies and climbing the ladder, whilst picking up a healthy pay cheque each month, owning fancy gadgets and driving fancy cars. Michael lived a life many people dream about. Like I say, a true success story; on the outside, that is.

Although he didn't appreciate it at the time, Michael now looks back and knows he was never happy. He didn't like the long hours. He didn't enjoy working for an hourly rate. It's easy to realise where you went wrong with hindsight, but much harder to understand it or see it at the time. Today, in many ways, Michael enjoys a similar lifestyle, but at the same time, not.

He makes good money and buys the gadgets he desires, but because he's the founder of *The Solopreneur Hour* (far more than a podcast, with speaking, coaching, and masterminds), he possesses the type of freedom he never realised he had craved.

This is where Stage Five: The Tipping Point becomes relevant, because it often takes a moment, a split second, an epiphany to pull you out of your slumber. Or, as you'll soon see, sometimes it takes a series of little epiphanies over a period of time; the 'Red Car Syndrome').

One of my favourite thinkers, Malcolm Gladwell, coined the term *'tipping point'* when he published his 2000 bestseller of the same name, *The Tipping Point*. He defines this as 'the moment of critical mass, the threshold, the boiling point.' It often describes the moment an idea or business takes off and booms, but for this book it refers to that moment of realisation… that split second… that epiphany of sorts.

The tipping point represents a positive period in your journey, because it's when you begin to see light at the end of your mistake or failure. It's when you overcome the depression and battle through the pain and the bargaining. It's when you see a new way forward, and a future that's far brighter than the past you previously knew.

'My mistake was staying longer than I should have,' said Michael, as he relaxed in an empty room, whilst his friend's conference (fellow *Successful Mistake* alumni, Nick Unsworth's) bustled to life in the same building. It's easy to say now with hindsight, but Michael only knew what he knew at the time. He wanted money and nice things, so he worked for impressive agencies. He wanted to climb the ladder because that's what you're supposed to do. But over the course of several months, Michael's life turned upside down, not only changing how he lived, but altering his entire perception of success forever.

'I lost both of my parents seven months apart from each other,' he said, describing an extremely painful period in his life. 'I lost everything. It literally bankrupted me, and I lost all the stuff I gained through my previous job and lifestyle.'

As you can imagine, Michael felt shock, pain and depression, not just because his parents passed, and not just because he lost all his money, but because so much change was thrust upon him. He needed to work and hustle and try harder to regain what he had, so he turned to a rather rich individual he'd connected with a few months prior. He needed a job. He needed help. This individual gave it him, but not in the way that Michael expected.

'I was still in the mindset of "can I work for him? Can I create a few websites for him? Can he give me a job of some kind?"' Michael said. 'But he flipped this mindset in an instant when I sat on his couch, because he said to me, "You know, Michael, I could help you and put you into a job where you earn $250k tomorrow, but you've suffered so much chaos in your life these last four months, you haven't had chance to mourn." At this very moment it dawned on me that my dad had died, that my mum had died, and that I'm human and I need to deal with this before I move on to anything else. I lost it on this guy's couch. One of my biggest goals was to send my parents on a European adventure, but they were now gone. Although I realised this didn't matter, because in this moment I decided I'd take them on this trip regardless.'

Michael spent the next four months travelling Europe and taking his parents ashes to all the places they'd dreamt of: The Vatican, Ireland (with a name like O'Neal, why not?), and a whole host more. When Michael told me this, I couldn't help but think he went through his version of depression on that guy's couch, and he needed to flee in order to find the clarity and strength to move forward.

By now, I hope you don't see a four-month trip like this as running away, but rather a chance to discover what's important. Michael did, and this tipping point changed everything.

'I returned from this experience with a new mindset, and a couple of poignant things happened. To begin with, I had $14 to my name. Period,' he said, laughing about how bleak his situation must have seemed from the outside. 'I realised that because I'd lost my mother so suddenly, I should say yes to every opportunity I could. I'd say yes first and figure out how to do it later. I also decided I'd never work an hour for a dollar again. And I never have since.'

Although this was a terribly hard period in his life, it brought perspective and meaning into Michael's living. It isn't that he didn't want the gadgets and the cars and the money, he just didn't want it whilst handcuffed to a business that asked him to work from early in the morning until late at night. But something else happened around this time that helped drum home this new outlook, and it's something that devastated the city of New Orleans and tore far too many families apart.

'I watched the aftermath of Hurricane Katrina on TV, and I remember thinking, "Of all the things that have gone wrong in my life of late — my parents passing, running out of money, and losing my job — I don't have it as bad as this." For so long I had compared up, wishing I had what others had, but all of a sudden I started to compare down — realising I have it better than so many other people in this world.'

My thirty-minute chat with Michael O'Neal changed me. I hated hearing his tale, because it isn't fair to lose the people you love, just like it isn't nice to hear about folk talk about losing their business or livelihood or passion. Mistakes and failure hurt, as does hardship, but they don't have to end you, nor do they have to define you — at least, not in a negative way.

Michael said his a-ha moment came on that couch, but I'm sure his tipping point had rumbled on for some time; as his parents grew sick, when they passed, as he travelled Europe with their ashes, watched the aftermath of a natural disaster on TV, and slowly realised he was never satisfied with the life he'd been living all along — a true case of Red Car Syndrome.

Maybe your own tipping point will come in an instant, inspiring you to take action and helping you see the light at the end of the tunnel. But maybe it will rumble on over a few weeks or months. It might not be a single a-ha moment that spurs you to take action, instead it could be lots of little ones; much like when you buy that new red car and you suddenly see lots of red cars just like yours, or the moment you find out you're going to be a parent, and all of a sudden there are babies everywhere.

You may not recognise this moment or appreciate it at the time, because we often require hindsight to understand such insights. But Stage Five: The Tipping Point is when you begin to transform your mistake and failure into success. It's the time you turn a good idea into a great one. It's when you pivot or start anew, building and working towards something far better. For Michael, this marinated within him for a few months before he knew what to do next, but for some it does happen in a flash. Which is where we'll begin, because those glorious lightbulb moments can shine so brightly.

YOUR LIGHTBULB MOMENT

As Michael O'Neal shows, your tipping point doesn't have to come in the form of a momentary epiphany. Several elements may form over weeks or months, encouraging you to take note or change or pivot. But sometimes your tipping point does come in a moment of lightbulbs and a-has, and we've already touched upon a few earlier in this book.

Jordan Harbinger had a shower and realised he was trying to come up with ways to keep a useless employee. Steve Olsher lost his stepfather and foresaw his own funeral. Chris Cerrone visited the doctor, who painted a rather clear picture of his future if he didn't change now.

You continue to learn and appreciate throughout your great mistake journey, so even when you suffer through shock, pain, bargaining, and depression, you learn more about yourself, your business, your idea, and what your next step should be. And sometimes this results in a single a-ha moment that ignites everything; you realise your mistake isn't the end of the world, and you see light at the end of the tunnel; you appreciate your idea and business, and think, 'We could do this, change that, pivot, grow…'

Who knows what your lightbulb moment will unearth, but it's often the beginning of something beautiful. It reinvigorates you and shows you a new way forward, like it did for Maggie Patterson when a long-time client offered her a new project she knew she would hate from the offset.

'I think the biggest mistake I made was getting complacent in my business,' Maggie said, a fellow storyteller and marketer who helps businesses reignite their brands through fresh communication. 'At the start of 2013, I took a step back and thought to myself, "what the hell am I doing?"'

Maggie's story resonates with a lot of others I've come across, because as you hopefully see by now, not all mistakes happen with a click of the fingers that brings your world to a standstill. Sure, this is sometimes the case, but they often manifest over longer periods of time. After all, Maggie lived a good life and did what she was supposed to, but bit by bit it ate away at her.

'I had a good income,' she said. 'I suppose I had everyone's dream job from the outside: working for myself, managing my schedule, living a life of freedom. But all I could think was, "this isn't success to me." I was unhappy. I wasn't stimulated. I just couldn't continue to live like that for another ten years.'

Maggie's mistake may have rumbled on for several years, but her tipping point hit her in a momentary epiphany as a magical lightbulb hovered above her head.

'I remember when it happened,' she said. 'I had this client who I loved. They were great, and they offered me this new high profile and lucrative program to manage. It would have been great for me to be involved in, but I couldn't be less inspired by the thought of working on it. I knew my role would be important and critical to their business, but the idea of me running it, oh my gosh, I couldn't do it. That's when I asked myself, "what the hell am I doing?"'

This moment, and rather simple question, opened Maggie's eyes. She took a step back, worked on some new training, and even took a trip to Fiji with her husband. She realised that although she worked for herself, managed her schedule, and lived a life of freedom, she didn't do so in a fashion that inspired or fulfilled her.

We laughed as she talked about not having a website at this point, but it hammered home the point that she helped her clients achieve success, but didn't take the time to figure out what success meant for her. She didn't practice what she preached, and all this led her to change the products and services she offered, tweak her client list, and begin working on projects that lit a fire within her.

'I've learned to check in with myself often and ask, "Am I

happy? Am I healthy? Am I doing what inspires me?"' she said. 'I have an idea what I'm doing this year and next, but I also appreciate that things may change. The difference today is, I'm conscious of the fact. I'm not simply going through the motions.'

What I took from my interview with Maggie was her newfound passion, because as she spoke to me, she did so with a particular pep that demonstrated how much she loved what she woke up to do each day. Before her tipping point, she did what she thought she had to do and remained blind to her issues. Once this lightbulb moment arrived, she unearthed new vigour in what she could offer her audience, and, of course, herself.

This entire stage — be it a momentary 'a-ha' (like Maggie's) or a prolonged journey (like Michael's) — guides you to ask different questions and look at your situation in a new light. It's when you begin to turn a good idea into a great one, alter and improve the products and services you offer, and pivot your business or approach so it connects with your audience; or, possibly even more important than this, so that it connects with *you* and makes you feel something. And when you're shown a new light like this, you may find your eyes open a little wider. You're able to look around and observe, as we see next, because if your lightbulb moment is what opens your eyes and forces you to ask important questions, the next step is figuring out the answers and seeking guidance from your customers, audience, friends, and more often than not, life.

It's time to open your eyes and ears, because it's doubtful you have all the answers yourself.

INSPIRED BY STORIES FROM: Maggie Patterson, ALBERT GREISMYER, JORDAN HARBINGER, DEBBIE MILLMAN, JIMMY VARLEY, JASON GRACIA, NATALIE SISSON, PETER HARRINGTON, STEVE OLSHER, BRIAN FOLEY, CLAY HEBERT, VERNON ROSS, JAMES SMITH, SEAN PLATT

OPEN YOUR EYES & EARS

You may think that a-ha moment will open your eyes and provide you with the answers, but I'm afraid the more likely outcome is further questions. After all, during Maggie Patterson's momentary epiphany she asked, 'What the hell am I doing?' Michael O'Neal turned to saying yes to opportunity, because he didn't have any other answer.

Your tipping point doesn't necessarily provide you with all the answers, but it is the time you escape the darkness and see that all-important light at the end of your tunnel. To uncover what this light has to offer, you are required to observe, and although you might imagine this involves surveys and asking your customers a whole host of questions, I encourage you to be patient.

I remember reading an article in which Brian Clark (the founder of Copyblogger and Rainmaker) said he didn't create products based on questionnaires or surveys, but rather by lurking on Copyblogger's comment section and paying attention to what people said. They gave him all the information he needed based on the questions they asked, the issues they faced, and the praise they offered, and it's much the same with your tipping point, because although you may now see your mistake in a brighter light, you may not appreciate the finer details just yet.

That's not to say that the finer details aren't around you at all times, just that you may have to open your eyes and ears to listen and observe. Sure, ask those 'bigger picture' questions and figure out what it is you want, but please, please, please don't forget about the world around you — your customers, your readers, your audience, your friends, your family, your peers, your mentors, those everyday snippets of life that pass you by.

In fact, you may find it's those everyday snippets that inspire you the most, because you're no longer stuck in a rut. You're no longer imprisoned by your mistake, instead you're excited to see where it could lead you. So, you observe the world with fresh eyes, which is what happened to Omar Zenhom and Nicole Baldinu of *$100 MBA* fame; a podcast that publishes ten-minute daily lessons for today's entrepreneur, a stark contrast to what the majority of other shows offer. But this wasn't always the case, as Omar explained:

'People kept asking us what our strategy for success was,' he said. 'And our answer to them each time was, "we failed!" This failure made us angry. It fuelled us. We wanted to succeed the next time around, and it's this that motivated us to do better.'

Like many others, Omar and Nicole slipped into that dreaded zone of conformity, because although they had an idea of what they wanted to produce, they didn't implement it on their own terms, instead focusing on an interview-based podcast because everyone seemed to find success this way, so why not them, too?

'Our first podcast didn't go well,' Omar continued. 'I mean, it was a good experience because we met lots of people we admired and learned a great deal, but in terms of a successful podcast that drove traffic and customers, it didn't do well at all.'

Finishing off each other's sentences, Nicole continued the tale. 'I began to think, "We're not using our strengths. We're focusing on the wrong thing, and worst of all, we're not enjoying it." I'd been a fan of the *Coffee Break* podcasts for years (podcasts that teach foreign languages in bite-sized chunks),' she said, 'So, I wondered if we could go back to what we were good at, which is education and reaching people.'

You see, both Nicole and Omar found entrepreneurship after a background in education. They were teachers who understood how to teach and inspire and simplify an issue, and all of a sudden they realised what their mistake had been all along.

'I figured, rather than do the interview-style podcast and be like everyone else, we could add value in a different way by creating a podcast that literally teaches entrepreneurs,' said Nicole, before passing the baton to Omar.

'Our outlook changed in an instant,' he said. 'We realised this format — short lessons that focus on something actionable — didn't exist for entrepreneurs. We knew we needed to stop doing what everyone else was and instead focus on something different, and something we are good at.'

Omar and Nicole initially conformed for the sake of conforming, an uncommon issue during an entrepreneur's early days. But this isn't the nugget to take from their tale, but rather how they realised they weren't taking advantage of their strengths, and by trying to be like everyone else, were setting themselves up for failure.

They overcame this by observing the world around them and piecing the puzzle together. There were a lot of podcasts that inspired and shared great interviews, but few that literally taught an entrepreneur important business lessons each day. There were also a lot of podcasts that lasted thirty minutes or longer, but too few that focused on the short and sweet end of the spectrum. They existed in other industries (The *Coffee Break* podcasts, for instance), but not for the time-strapped entrepreneur. Not only this, but the gap that existed in their market aligned perfectly with their expertise and background in education.

A-ha! Their eyes were opened! There was the glorious light at the end of the tunnel. But they didn't get to this tipping point by asking their audience questions or sending out a questionnaire. I'm not suggesting questionnaires or surveys don't work, but maybe observation is all you truly need. Because had Omar and Nicole asked their audience what they wanted from the show, they would more than likely be given the obvious answers; quality, type of guest, frequency, and so on. Instead, they observed their world, considered their strengths and what they could bring to the table, placed themselves in their fellow entrepreneur's shoes, and opened their eyes and ears. The answer they searched for appeared out of thin air.

It's difficult to say who will provide you the right answer during your tipping point. Maybe it's your customer. Maybe it's your peers. Maybe it's within you as you consider what your own pain points are, and place yourself in other people's shoes. Maybe it's sitting in a coffee shop as you watch life pass you by. Whatever it is, it begins by opening your eyes and ears, and observing the world around you.

I like to think that the entire journey of your great mistake provides valuable lessons and insights, but I personally love this tipping point stage the most because it's when light is borne out of the darkness of pain, shock and depression. It's when you turn the corner and realise that this mistake will not define you. It's marvellous, but just because this new realisation and appreciation ignites (*be it momentary or prolonged*), it doesn't mean it provides you with the answers you need to take your next step forward.

But once you open your eyes and take it all in, a whole new world presents itself. More often than not, it's where you best idea yet resides.

INSPIRED BY STORIES FROM: OMAR ZENHOM, NICOLE BALDINU, CORBETT BARR, DAVE URSILLO, JOHN CORCORAN, JON CRAWFORD, LINDSEY RAINWATER, LUKE HUDSON, MARIANNE CANTWELL, RICK TIELMAN, MIKE TIELMAN, TOM GREVERSEN, DAVE CONREY, DESIREE EAST, ETHAN AUSTIN, JARED EASLEY, JEFF GOINS, BERNADETTE JIWA, MARK MANSON, JARED EASLEY

YOUR NEW OUTLOOK AWAITS

So far in Stage Five: The Tipping Point, you've uncovered a-ha moments, lights at the end of the tunnel, and the importance of opening your eyes and observing the world around you. This process can take time or happen all at once, but whatever your circumstances, it tends to lead to one outcome; a new outlook on business, life, success and ultimately you.

It's why I love this stage the most, because it's when you begin to transform your mistake into success; where you turn failure and hardship into something life-changing and earth shifting. It truly can lead you to greatness, and although we'll focus on this in greater detail within Stage Six: Reconstruction, I'd like to touch upon it now, because it's during this stage that your new outlook begins to form. After all, it's during their tipping point that Omar and Nicole transformed the *$100 MBA* podcast into what it is today, and like Omar himself said, 'It was during this period our outlook changed in an instant.'

I liken it to struggling with a puzzle for hours on end, unable to see the answer through the maze and chaos, only to see it as clear as day once someone points it out to you.

This new outlook could present a new product or service or idea; a new or altered business model, maybe; or a simple pivot of what you already do; or possibly, a complete reinvention of your business and brand. This new outlook may focus on you as a person, or your company's overall culture. This new outlook can come in so many forms, but it's here where your glorious #greatmistake is often born. It's when you transform an okay idea into a great one. It's when you turn good money into life-changing amounts. It's when you establish something memorable and meaningful, and although it can lead to a completely new business, often it requires a slight tweak here and a small adjustment there. For instance, when I spoke to Pamela Slim, she spoke about such a tweak and adjustment.

A bestselling author, world-renowned speaker, authority blogger, and all-round all-star, Pam's mistake didn't place her on the brink of extinction or even threaten what she built. In many ways, her mistake is a nice one to have, for it grew out of growth, success and popularity. But it affected her nevertheless, and led her to a tipping point that changed her outlook on her business, and what her business means to her. Without this new outlook, she wouldn't be doing what she does today.

'I'm a community builder by nature,' Pam said, describing how important connecting with people and forming relationships is to her. 'I love to be serving people and connecting with them, but I found this could become a limiting factor. I spent a lot of time and placed a lot of my resources into individuals, and individual projects where there wasn't a lot of leverage. Don't get me wrong, this did present a lot of joy because I was able to form great relationships with those I worked with, but I could only work on so much and with so many at any one time.'

Growing your business is tough, and although Pam found herself in a great position where people wanted more of her, she realised she reached a ceiling of sorts, and more worryingly, saw her focus on quality falter.

'I had this one client,' she continued, 'and after working with her for a while she said, "I feel like I need you to be more connected with my business, not just when we speak." This made me stop and think about what I was doing, and it was an uncomfortable moment because I wanted to serve everybody in the same way, but I can only do so much. It was a good wake up call, and one I absolutely needed.'

Pam was not only stifling her growth, but she began to damage how she served her clients; the aspect that set her apart to begin with. She realised in an instant that she needed to think about the future and find a new way of working that suited her lifestyle and her values (relationships, connection, serving people), whilst fulfilling her family's needs, too.

'I realised I had to create some parameters where I could reach one-to-many,' she said. 'This new outlook actually became a driving force behind my book, *The Body of Work,* because I needed to focus on actions and tools that scale more easily. This was hard because I started to say no to coaching, which I loved, but I had to focus on reaching more people with what I do, whilst remaining true to what's important to me.'

You may consider oversubscribing to work and reaching your ceiling to be a nice mistake to make, but it's a mistake that still breeds stress, pain, and hardship. Pam had a business model that worked and provided a service that people valued, but she outgrew it.

It's not a negative thing by any means, but it isn't the fact that Pam realigned and tweaked her business that's important here, but rather her new outlook on how she had to scale her future ideas so they could reach more people and help them in a way that remained true to her values.

'I think each person, at each stage in their life, can find the perfect business model to suit them,' Pam said.

I love this. The fact that Pam adjusted her way of working isn't what stands out to me, it's her realisation that her business model may change as her own situation and wants and needs do. As her kids grow older, maybe her outlook will shift. If more people visit her site and buy her books, maybe she'll have to tweak how she serves them and communicates with them.

All this is fine, because Pam's ready for whatever awaits her, and it's this new outlook that allows her to scale her ideas and grow her business, all the while maintaining those all-important values. She didn't have to reinvent herself, but she did have to leave behind coaching and tweak how she worked. Pam's new outlook didn't require a huge shift or a completely new business, whereas maybe yours will. Maybe yours will lead you to a completely new idea or direction, or general shift that turns your world upside down.

The point isn't what this new outlook leads you to do, it's how it helps you appreciate what you do, how you do it, why you're doing it, and that you do the right thing for you, your audience, and those that matter to *you*.

Your tipping point opens your eyes, and often gives you all the answers and realisations that you need in order to move into Stage Six: Reconstruction, where you literally transform your mistake into success. But before we leave the tipping point behind us, there's one last thing we need to visit, and it just so happens to focus on you.

INSPIRED BY STORIES FROM: PAMLEA SLIM, ALBERT GREISMYER, CLAUD WILLIAMS, DANNY FEIN, DAVE URSILLO, EVO TERRA, JAiMIE Masters, JIMMY VARLEY, JOANNA PENN, JON CRAWFORD, MICHALE O'NEAL, ROSS KEMP, CESAR ABEID, JEFF GOINS, BERNADETTE JIWA, ELLORY WELLS, GARY BUTTERFIELD TABITHA NAYLOR, TEMI KOLEOWO, JAMES SMITH

IT'S TIME TO FOCUS ON YOU!

Throughout this successful mistake adventure, we've focused on your personal wellbeing. We keep returning to this because you, your health, and your emotional state remains the most important piece of the puzzle at all times, because you're nothing without your health. How can you and your business function if you don't ensure *you* function properly?

Although the tipping point is mostly a happy and positive period, full of optimism, new outlooks, and an added skip to your step, it's easy to get caught up in these new realisations, neglect you and your wellbeing, and unfortunately, slip back to where you just came from.

Now, I don't know about you, but the thought of creating a new mistake at this stage of the process, all because you get lost within yourself seems a little silly. So be sure to take some time to focus on you before you begin reconstructing your empire in Stage Six.

You've already met people like Chris Cerrone and Ari Meisel, folk whose mistakes were borne out of neglecting their health. Out of all of the patterns I've uncovered throughout this book-writing adventure, it's health that creates the biggest 'sit up and realise what the hell you're doing to yourself' moment. Take Jenny Blake, for instance, the author, speaker, coach, and epic yoga teacher whose smile has the power to inspire you in a millisecond. Once upon a time, Jenny worked at Google, in the type of role many folk dream about. She loved her time there, loved the culture, and so much more, but surprising to nobody, she worked and worked, holding her health prisoner all the while.

'The biggest mistake I've made was treating my body like the enemy,' Jenny said, telling me about her Google experience, the long hours, the fact that she took medication but didn't change her lifestyle. Then the time came when she left her job to start her own business, and live a life built on freedom, but she decided to take a trip to the doctor's office beforehand; you know, just to touch base and check in.

'I sat across from this rather gruff and intimidating doctor,' she said, 'and he told me I should take this pill that would kill and replace my thyroid, therefore removing my problem. I'd have to take this pill the rest of my life, but I'd be okay because my problem would disappear. He was such a bully about it, and I remember thinking to myself, "Hell no! I'm not going to kill an organ in my body." It's then that I realised that maybe my body wasn't out to get me, rather to warn me. So, I went against the doctor's orders and slept more, ate better, and exercised every day. It's been three and a half years, and I haven't had any issues since.'

Jenny's overactive thyroid wasn't necessarily linked to stress of the corporate grind, but she mentioned several times how she intrinsically believed that it played an important role. And as soon as she took a step back, slept longer, did yoga on a regular basis, and changed how she approached her work and general day, her health transformed dramatically. If you take a look at her site and yoga skills, this is a woman who today is in good shape and good health. A few years ago, not so much.

Still, this section isn't about you overworking, over-stressing, or falling victim to this disease or that, it's about taking a moment to focus on you for a few minutes; not your business. You've just overcome the shock, pain, bargaining, and depression, and you now stand before the entrepreneurial world with new and fresh ideas.

You're ready to go forward and transform your mistake into success, and it's easy to get carried away and throw yourself in whole-heartedly, possibly forgetting what caused your initial mistake and failure to begin with. But here's the thing, your health matters; *you* matter. As an entrepreneur, you may have a tendency to be 'on it' at all times. When an idea strikes, or when a launch edges near, you're into it one hundred percent. That's good. Well done. Your success often depends on this. But you don't have to neglect everything else whilst you do so.

'I'm not saying we should all take naps each day and never work,' Jenny said, 'because there are going to be hectic times when you have to step up and get things done; work those long days. But I think where a lot of entrepreneurs fall short is ensuring they find enough time to recover from this. It's about shifting your mindset so you appreciate that when you slow down, your mind doesn't stop. You'll still come up with ideas. You'll continue to come up with solutions. You'll still do a great job, even if you're not working at one hundred miles an hour.'

And before I say anything else, I'm guilty of this too. When my tipping point comes calling, I find myself over-excited and adding too much to my to-do list; stressing out like I have two days to live and a lifetime to fit it all into. It's understandable, because this is your baby. This is your business. This is your dream, your freedom, your idea and your life.

It's easy to slip back into your mistake before you truly escape it, but that's not to say you have to. You can fight it, resist it, and all it takes is for you to take a step back and focus on *you* for a few minutes.

The tipping point, like Stage Six: Reconstruction, is an exciting time full of hope and possibility, and after all the doom and gloom of pain, shock and depression, it's a fantastic stage to find yourself in. Just be sure to place your health and wellbeing at the top of your priorities, because without you, what the hell are you left with?

And so we leave Stage Five: The Tipping Point behind, and venture forward into Stage Six: Reconstruction. You learn plenty about you and your business throughout this entire great mistake journey, but it's at this point when things truly turn around.

But you're not there yet! There's still work to do before you transform your faux pas into a glorious success story, but you edge ever closer. I'm excited to share this stage with you, as well as some inspiring individuals who rose from the ashes. But before we do, let's end Stage Five: The Tipping Point in style, and recap the key learnings as well a few tasks that are sure to set you on the right path.

INSPIRED BY STORIES FROM: AJ LEON, JENNY BLAKE, ARI MEISEL, KATE MATS, LINSI BROWNSON, JAYSON GAIGNARD, CHRIS SANDS, ALAN KIPPING-RUANE, BRIAN HORN, KATE NORTHRUP

STAGE 5: TASKS & TAKEAWAYS

The following recaps what you've just read, sums up the main learnings, and provides a few actionable tasks you can implement into your world today. You can also download a free version of this workbook at: successfulmistake.com/takeaways

TOP TEN TAKEAWAYS FROM STAGE 5

1) **The tipping point** is when you begin to transform your mistake and failure into success, and is the time that you start to see the light at the end of the tunnel.

2) Sometimes this comes in a single **lightbulb moment**, where something happens, someone says something, you visit someplace, or you simply sit back and say a-ha, as everything clicks into place.

3) However, this tipping point can take several weeks or months before it makes sense to you, creeping up on you bit by bit in a strong case of **Red Car Syndrome** — where lots of people say something, you see lots of somethings, and after a while, you're finally ready to listen; or it finally feels relevant to you.

4) Your tipping point rarely offers answers, but rather a chance to **open your eyes** and take notice of what's around you; people, ideas, opportunities, processes, alternatives…

5) When you **open your eyes** and take in your

surroundings, you may be surprised as to how many answers begin to present themselves, which allows you to move into Stage Six: Reconstruction.

6) This opening of your eyes also brings a **new outlook** into your world, because you suddenly begin to see your mistakes and failures (not just this one, but those in the past) in a new and far more positive light.

7) This **new outlook** not only provides you with the power to transform failure into success, but helps you apply a more successful and positive mindset moving forward.

8) But your tipping point also offers a potential warning, because during the excitement and new hope of success, you can **lose focus** and rush the process, making certain rash decisions that rekindle your mistake all over again.

9) A good way to overcome this is to **focus on you** and your health, and ensure you don't work too much, too fast, or to an extent where you're harming your physical and mental wellbeing.

10) Although your **tipping point** rarely provides you with many answers, it's this stage where everything you're about to create forms, and it's here where you begin to see the true positives in your mistakes and failures.

~ () ~

TOP TASKS FROM STAGE 5

1) Consider a difficult period in your past *(a break-up, death in the family, failed business, etc.),* that you have since recovered from.

2) Spend twenty minutes thinking about this difficult period, in particular the time when everything began to get easier. Re-living this past tipping point, make notes of everything you felt, the people you spoke to, the places you visited, and anything else that springs to mind. There's no right or wrong answer, simply write what comes to mind.

3) Based on this list, focus on the moment or moments you believe acted as your tipping point, and led you to see the light at the end of the tunnel.

4) Finally, using this past tipping point as an inspiration, as well as what you learned during Stage Five, write about what you can apply today, and how you can use this to better open your eyes, observe what's around you, and focus on yourself to ensure you see the glorious light at the end of the tunnel.

On their own, these tasks may seem strange, but as you work through this book you'll begin to appreciate how these actionable sections help you implement what you've just learned straight away.

Because remember, this book isn't here to simply inspire and entertain you, but also <u>educate</u> you at the same time.

And to make your life easier, you can download an interactive version of these Tasks & Takeaways, which lets you make notes within the PDF itself (and print it off), as well as watch a video tutorial where I go through each task one by one, and explain how and why they are relevant to you in the here-and-now.

Download your worksheet at: <u>successfulmistake.com/takeaways</u>

INTRODUCING OUR CHAPTER PARTNER,
SCRIVENER

Hello, my name is David, and I'm one of the directors at Literature & Latte, the company behind Scrivener: the powerful content generation tool for writers that allows you to concentrate on composing and structuring long and difficult documents.

When Matthew first told me about The Successful Mistake, I couldn't wait to hear more, let alone read the book and uncover all the stories from the entrepreneurs he'd interviewed. It covers a theme we can all learn from, and as a company we were excited to support Matthew and be part of The Successful Mistake journey.

Then Matthew asked me to introduce Stage Six: Reconstruction, and talk about a mistake we made whilst building Scrivener. It took me a few days to choose one, because as I'm sure you can imagine, we've made several over the years.

However, one particular mistake stands out above the rest, and it's one we're continuing to work through as I write these words, despite the fact this situation began almost five years ago. It surrounds our Scrivener on iOS app, which aims to take all the main features of Scrivener that you use on your computer, onto your iPad and iPhone. It has become our largest project with regard to time taken and sleepless nights, and only came about as our existing customers kept asking us to build it. We cannot wait to release the app, as we know it will help a lot of writers, but we do wish we'd gone about things rather differently.

For starters, we announced the development of Scrivener for iOS in December 2011, and although we didn't have an exact release date in mind, we thought it would only take months; maybe a year at most. This was the start of our great mistake, because it placed needless pressure on us at a time when we were still figuring out the inner workings of the app.

Luckily for us, we have an amazing customer base who have supported us throughout, and shown a great deal of patience. But still, we know how excited they are about this product, and we hate the fact that it's taken so long to deliver on our announcement.

So, why has this app taken so long in the first place? This is where our next big mistake came to be, as we trusted third-party developers too much. Over the five years, we involved several freelance developers, each time placing trust in them to build the app per our specifications, and to do so in a timely fashion.

Our first developer was beset with a personal issue, and we sympathised with her loss of focus for the project. We eventually had to move on and bring a second developer on board, who repeatedly failed to meet our expectations.

We'd wasted a lot of time and investment at this point, so we tackled the issue head-on and involved several 'specialist' developers from a London based agency, but again, this turned out to simply waste more time and finances. We were still a long way from achieving what we wanted, and all of this led us to realise something very important: if we were to create the app we wanted, we needed to bring the development in-house and trust our own skillsets.

After all, it was these that built Scrivener in the first place, and considering this is arguably our most involved project to date, it makes sense that we are the ones building it.

None of this makes wasting vast swathes of time easier, but we now have confidence in what we can produce and who we are as a company more than ever before. The truth is, we placed trust in others when we should have placed it in ourselves. We had sound reasons for doing this, in not wanting to dilute our focus on our client based versions of Scrivener, but if we had taken the primary role earlier, it's safe to say Scrivener on iOS would be available now.

So, when Matthew talks about Reconstruction during the

following pages, I can personally relate a great deal. We went through our own tipping point, and we developed a new outlook on who we are and what we have to offer. Like I say, it doesn't make the lost time unimportant, but we're solely focussed on the future now, and we're excited about what it holds.

We're reconstructing our greatest mistake as we speak, and we couldn't be happier. Soon, Scrivener will be available on iOS, and we believe it will be far better than we could have originally achieved. Going through phases of failure with other developers helped us hone what we wanted to produce. I feel this demonstrates the power of mistakes and failure, which is what Matthew has dedicated this entire book around.

As such, I'm excited to introduce Stage Six: Reconstruction, and hand you back to Matthew who has more inspiring stories to share with you.

RECONSTRUCT

STAGE 6: **THE BEGINNING OF YOUR #GREATMISTAKE**

As I logged on to Skype, a colourful scene unfolded before my eyes; her blonde hair and Australian smile, flowers and festive bunting dotting the background, with hints of yellow throughout the room. Marianne Cantwell introduced herself before we jumped into a conversation like the two of us were lifelong friends.

Comfortable in her skin, and with an effortless charm that fills you with ease, it's little wonder that Marianne's built a thriving community of *Free Range Humans;* folk eager to escape their corporate shackles and build a life on their own terms.

I thought I had Marianne figured out in an instant, and although I didn't know what her greatest mistakes would be, I couldn't imagine it would revolve around insecurity, conformity, and struggling to know what value she had to share with the world. After all, this is how she helps her *Free Range Humans* each day; but that's the funny thing about mistakes and failure, and it's something we can all forget about from time to time. You see a successful person, someone comfortable in what they do and thriving because of it, and assume this is how it's always been.

You forget they struggled through their own journey, and you forget they may continue to struggle with issues within. Which I suppose is the whole point of this book and the #greatmistake journey you're on, because it isn't about clinging to the past and the faux pas you've made, it's about learning from them, pushing through them, and coming out on top of them. Chin held high, shoulders firm.

In Stage Six: Reconstruction, your great mistake begins to reform. That tipping point shines new light on your situation and world, and you're able to rebuild or start again or change course. It's here that you grow and transform a bad situation into a life-changing one, and soon enough you'll sit on a Skype call with someone like me interviewing you, as I presume you've had it all figured out from the beginning. I did this with Marianne, because I figured it was impossible that such a colourful, happy, and in-control individual could once have suffered through insecurity and conformity.

'When I quit my job in 2008,' Marianne said, wrapped in a bright yellow scarf, 'I did every single sensible thing I could think of. I read the books. I got the website. I designed the logo and created a solid business plan, and I went in search of clients, but I focused so hard on looking and being professional, that I ended up with zero. The mistake I made was assuming that if you look professional, you get paid for it. But I think this is something a lot of people fall into in the beginning, and when you're struggling. You look at what other people do, what their websites look like, and what their language is. You think, "if I can replicate this but make it a little better, surely I'll find success."'

Marianne made the type of mistake most new entrepreneurs do. It's scary in the beginning, and although you want to pave your own path, it's easier said then done. Copying someone else and doing everything you're supposed to seems much safer. But it's not, and you don't need me to tell you how important it is to embrace *you*, your personality, and what you offer the world that nobody else can. Regardless, it remains a common mistake most entrepreneurs make, and it's one that set Marianne back several months. Yet at the same time, it was this that set her on the right path.

'I realised after a few months that I'd entirely removed myself and my personality from the business,' she said. 'I didn't have any pictures of me on my website. I removed my language and style. I'd taken out any fun elements, and basically stripped away everything about me in order become the person I thought I should be. My biggest mistake was assuming that my personality and style was something to be hidden, whereas it's this that sets me apart.'

After a few months of trying to fit in and getting nowhere, Marianne touched upon her own tipping point, a period that set the foundations for the world she thrives in today. It didn't happen overnight. Nor did she come up with every answer in an instant. But she recognised her shortcomings and set out to reconstruct her business and life in a way only she could.

'I turned this around,' she continued. 'I thought about what makes me me, and the areas in which I tend to find success. I totally revamped everything. At this stage in time, I was doing one-on-one work with people, helping them focus on their CV writing and how to get a job — rather ironic when you consider what *Free Range Humans* is all about today. I changed this, and instead started to do group work and workshops. I began to blog, and it didn't take long to realise that the more videos I uploaded, the more of *my* language I used, and the more of *my* personality I shared, the more people wanted to work with me. I left behind the old brand and fully embraced *Free Range Humans*. After a while it morphed into a community that helped people find themselves, escape their job, and build a life on their own terms — instead of helping them find and keep a job in the first place."

And this is what led Marianne to write her own book, travel the world, meet lots of amazing people, and live the life she continues to live today. She reconstructed her world after realising she'd made mistakes, and it was during this stage she transformed her failure into something more.

Stage Six: Reconstruction differs from one entrepreneur to the next. For some it involves starting afresh as you leave one brand behind and craft another out of its ashes. For others it requires focus, honing in on what you do and a refusal to get distracted by anything else. For you, it may involve expanding your business, going all in, hiring new team members, and taking your growth to the next level. Or maybe it requires a little diversification or a pivot of sorts. This is how you'll spend the rest of this stage, unravelling the stories from those who reconstructed their businesses and transformed their mistakes into success.

Through **focus**, **expansion**, **diversification**, or **starting again**, this is when you turn things around. This is your time to right some wrongs and push your mistakes, failure, and all that hardship behind you. It's time to take those lessons learnt and put them to action. It's time to construct your #greatmistake and stride forward with your head held high, and more often than not, this requires you to focus on what you're already doing, and refine instead of branching out and spreading your wings.

FΩCUS

I don't know what constitutes an entrepreneur these days, but because you read this book I presume you are one, wish to be one, or at least live a life where you control your daily life (as a freelancer, artist, creative, writer, blogger, or such). Because of this, it may be difficult for you to focus, because there are so many ideas swarming your mind, and you come across new opportunities and meet new people each day. Added to that, you want to grow and spread your wings, and no matter how rich or infamous you become, you'll no doubt want to keep moving forward forever. Why else would you read a book like this, after all?

Because of your nature, it's nigh on impossible to focus at all times. I'm terrible at it. I try to concentrate my attentions, narrow things down and stop myself from starting a new project, but I'm always distracted by, 'what if I did this'. In fact, I love creating new ideas so much that I often forget to sell the products that lie at the end of them, filling my day with so much work that when I look back at the end of it I wonder what I've achieved.

Does this sound familiar? Of course it does. You're a born entrepreneur and a self-made person. And here's the double-edged sword, because one of the biggest issues about making mistakes and failing in the first place is that it ruffles your feathers. You've just read entire sections on shock, pain, bargaining, and depression, and although after reading this book you'll be in a better position to control and overcome these, you'll still go through them. These mistakes and failures will continue to ruffle your feathers, because however successful or experienced you are, nobody's immune to such pressure.

And, like all entrepreneurs, when your feathers are ruffled, you tend to try compensate with more, more, more; an issue we've already delved into, with the likes of Francis Pedraza.

Each entrepreneur reconstructs their journey differently, but the most common response during this adventure of interviews was *focus.* Overall, entrepreneurs tend to spread themselves far too thinly. You lose focus on what matters and what your goal is, because everything else vies for your attention. But when people come across their all-important tipping point and take a little time to step back and figure out what the right answer is, they tend to realise they need to delve deeper into what they're already doing. Concentrate on what's important. Go all-in on that single idea. Don't create a new product or service or attempt to tackle a new industry, instead, master what you're already doing; truly serve your customers; blow the existing ones away before you search for an army of new ones; be better at what you do, perfect it; above all, ensure you validate everything you offer.

Validation is another word I've come across a lot, and one that goes hand in hand with focus. Often, it isn't that your idea/product/project/service is bad, it's that you try to move too quickly, do too much, or approach it from the wrong angle. Focus and validation force you to dive deeper into what you're doing and concentrate on what truly matters. You may even find yourself asking a rather simple question like 'is this what my customer actually needs?' And if you're unable to answer this then you may have a problem. When I spoke to Grant Baldwin, he talked about such validation and focus.

An already renowned professional speaker, Grant found rapid success online when he launched his podcast, *How Did You Get Into That*. With a growing list of subscribers and followers, Grant looked for new ways to provide them value through courses and products, but it's only after a disastrous launch that he's now able to give them what they need.

'Whilst speaking at schools,' he said, on a late September afternoon. 'I heard from a lot of students and parents who wanted help organising and understanding their finances ahead of college. So, we listened and put together a course, spent a lot of time on it, and by the end we thought we had this perfect product that everyone would love. But when the big launch day arrived there was nothing. I was thinking we might make

$10,000 or $15,000 in the first week, but we ended up making $700.'

I know Grant's pain, and I imagine you do too. When a new idea forms, especially one borne from actual customer feedback, you move forward with pace and excitement, and create the best product you can. But unless you know for sure, you don't know anything at all.

'The biggest issue we had was our buyers and audience were different people,' Grant said. 'I was speaking to students because I wanted them to take ownership and desire the product, but realistically it was their parents who would buy it. We were divided, sometimes communicating to the students and other times their parents, and so I think we created a lot of confusion. I suppose we were divided ourselves, too, undecided as to who the course was for.'

Recognising his shortcomings, Grant was keen to ensure such a launch would never happen again, so when it came to constructing these new courses and products for their ever-growing podcast audience, he took a completely new approach.

'A lot of the time we build products by going into our cave, building and creating, and then coming out and selling them,' he said. 'By doing this, all you do is build something and hope for the best. The mistakes made during this initial course helped me perfect the process I undertake today. These days, rather than me going into my cave and creating something, we form a test group of people who sign up and pay for it, but I tell them from the beginning, "There is no course yet. You're buying thin air. But we'll work on this together and create something you need, rather than me creating something *I* think you do."'

It wasn't that Grant created a bad course for these students, or that it was a bad idea, either. The course itself wasn't the mistake, it was how he approached it; but when you fail in this regard, it's bound to ruffle your feathers and force your entrepreneurial mind into a tail spin where you want to do more, hustle, go bigger, go faster. You quickly try a new audience or move on to your next idea and build a new project and go, go, go. But steady your horses; let's think this through. Grant realised it wasn't this initial course that was the issue, simply the fact he didn't take the time to validate it. As he said himself, 'I suppose we were divided ourselves, too, undecided as to who the course was for.'

Grant's divided focus meant that he had a product that was neither one thing nor another, so the way to overcome this mistake was to focus, dive deeper, concentrate on what he was good at and ensure it fulfilled his audiences' desires. In other words, he needed to unite his team and make sure everyone knew what they were creating and who they were creating it for.

These days, Grant may create different courses and products for a different type of audience, but it's this approach of focus and validation that allows him to build one success after another, and help those he serves build their own speaking empire. Had he sat down with a friend and shared the story behind this failed launch, they may have said something along the lines of 'that was a bad idea. You'd better not do that again. Maybe you should try something else, instead.' With his feathers already ruffled, Grant may have agreed and tried something new, branched out, diversified, or moved on to the next idea or venture. But as you know, it wasn't that the idea wasn't a good one, it just needed greater focus, more validation, and better understanding of what he could offer and what his audience needed.

This is an all too familiar story for me. I sit here typing these words as a man whose gut reaction for far too long was to fail, panic, and make matters worse by moving on to the next idea and simply drawing a line under whatever I started as a failure. I would say to myself, 'that was a bad idea. Better not do that again.' I was wrong, because it's focus that often gets you through.

It's by far the most common reaction within the many interviews I've undertaken for this book, and the more inspiring and successful people I meet, not just in business, but all walks of life, the more I personally appreciate the value of focus.

But what if you're unable to focus and explore what you're doing? What if you do have to branch our and spread your wings, because you know staying on the same course won't get you to where you want to be? Well, I'm glad you asked, because that's where we're heading to next.

INSPIRED BY STORIES FROM: GRANT BALDWIN, ARNOLD DU TOIT, DAVE CURSILLO, CHRIS BROGAN, DEAN PHILLIPS, ERIN BLASKIE, GREG SMUK, LIAM PATTERSON, LINDA COLES, RAMEET CHAWLA, SHARON HERMON, SHEILA VIERS, TEA SILVESTRE, ZEKE CAMUSIO, DANA HUMPHREY, JOANNA DAVIES

DIVERSIFY

Although focusing on what you're already doing is often the best way to transform your mistakes into success, sometimes you need to broaden your horizons and diversify. This could be a slight deviation or a large one, because remember, this is your journey and your #greatmistake, so where one individual needs to focus, you may have to completely step out of that comfortable circle you've built for yourself. Diversifying can include new products, new ideas, or an extension of what you already produce.

You may actually find your mistake teaches you so much about you and your business that you couldn't possibly confine yourself to where you currently are. Take this book, for instance, and the larger than life entity it's taken that expands far beyond the reaches of these pages. As you can imagine, I've made plenty of mistakes and stumbled over many obstacles whilst writing and publishing this book, and I've gone through my own version of a #greatmistake. I've learned a great deal, and one of the most important things is how this book cannot and should not remain a mere book.

Simply put, there's so much to share with you; so much more than I ever could have predicted when I first set out on this adventure, that had I kept adding to the pages and making it longer and more in-depth, I'd not only ruin the narrative and flow, but limit the amount of people I could reach and serve, because not everyone gets everything they need from a book. Some people want more, and some require a more one-on-one approach. As such, I realised I'd have to diversify this idea, so this book lead to an offshoot of other books that focus on individual interviews and stories. It encouraged me to produce workbooks, events, speaking engagements, online workshops, further interviews, a course, and a community of like-minded individuals who wish to understand what success means to them. This has led to lots of new ideas, and a programme that continues to evolve each week.

If I'd focused on this book and nothing else, I'd have limited the value that I could have offered incredible folk like you. I'd also have limited the amount of people I could have reached with my work, and worst of all, ruined the book itself by making it far too long and boring. So, although focusing and going all in on your idea is often the best path to take, it doesn't always serve you best. I had to diversify my own idea and branch out in the pursuit of fulfilling both mine and my idea's potential, much like Danny Fein, the founder of Litographs, a company that creates beautiful book-related products.

This in itself isn't rare or special, because there are lots of businesses that create book-related products, but because Litographs' designs integrate the entire text of a book into their artwork, they produce something quite remarkable. You have to see them to appreciate how great they are. When I sat down to speak to Danny, it was hot on the heels of his first successful crowdfunding campaign, which I'm happy to say surpassed all expectations. But after Danny shared the tricky beginnings his company had experienced, I realised it hadn't been an easy journey throughout.

'When we started out, we created poster designs for our first seven books and launched at this outdoor street market in Washington DC,' Danny said, describing the exciting time when he turned his idea into reality. 'We decided to print one hundred copies of each design, so we had an initial run of seven hundred posters. I was rather optimistic, to be honest, and thought we might sell out during this opening weekend, but although it went well and we received fantastic feedback, we returned home with around five hundred posters. I still had a full-time job at this point, I lived in a small apartment with no office space, and I was left with all these posters. This was bad for a few reasons: First of all, it was expensive to print them because we were still figuring out the logistics and finer details; second, it was difficult to store and keep the posters in good condition, which lead to a lot of wasted posters. But the third and most important issue of all was that we didn't have the resources to expand our collection of book designs, which we've since discovered is our most important area of growth.'

Now, most businesses that sell actual products go through teething problems like this. You either buy too much stock or too little, and both avenues can affect your growth. But this initial mistake taught Danny a lot, and rather than it leading him to focus on what they already offered, it forced him to branch out and broaden his horizons. It led him to appreciate how more designs meant greater choice, and that this results in far happier customers. It also helped him to see that they wouldn't have to settle for posters, and that increasing the number of book designs wouldn't be the only way they could branch out.

'This mistake helped us to learn a lot,' he said. 'Beyond helping us gauge what demand was like for each poster, it helped us to create the strategy that defines our success today; to utilise pre-ordering to grow our audience and increase our collection — not just for posters, but for new product lines altogether.'

Enter Kickstarter and the other successful campaigns Litographs have launched for their t-shirts and temporary tattoos.

When I spoke to Danny, they were focused on posters and had just begun to pre-launch their t-shirts. As I write this, their poster collections and t-shirts have boomed, leaving Danny and his team to diversify into tote bags and temporary tattoos, among other ideas in the pipeline. Their designs remain awesome; their style and approach to detail, the same. But this initial mistake of ordering too many posters taught Danny two important lessons:

- ✓ How valuable pre-ordering is

- ✓ That diversifying and branching-out (both with design and products) held the key to their success.

The truth is, you'll often have to focus on and fine tune what you already do in order to turn failure into success, but there are occasions where doing so doesn't only make matters worse, but leads to the end of you and your dream.

Sometimes, you do have to broaden your horizons, diversify what you offer, and branch out into new markets and product lines, just like Danny did with Litographs, and just as I have for *The Successful Mistake*. Your situation is your situation, and your journey differs to everyone else. Own it, and let your own tipping point guide the way, because once you open your eyes you can make sure you uncover the right answer. After all, who knows you and your business better than you?

Although sometimes focus or diversification isn't the way to go, because maybe you need to double up and expand, which is not only a scary and intimidating thought, but one that has the power to make or break you. Still, it's often where your greatest successes lie, which is where we turn our attention next.

INSPIRED BY STORIES FROM: DANNY FEIN, ALEXANDRA FRANZEN, MAGGIE PATTERSON, MARIANNE CANTWELL

EXPAND

You don't need me to tell you how important growth is. If you're not striding forward and setting new challenges for you and your business, you may as well be going backwards.

Of course, growth comes in many guises, and sometimes something counter intuitive like focusing and finding your niche is the best way to ensure it happens. Sometimes, though, you do need to expand your operations and spread your wings, and although such expansion can come in the form of diversifying, like it did for Danny and the Litographs team, it often comes down to you doing what you already do, but on a far grander scale. For instance, maybe your mistake entails keeping everything you do in-house, so you expand by outsourcing more of your operations to agencies and third parties. Maybe you personally bite off more than you can chew and slip into bad health, which leads you to expand your team and hire new people. Maybe you waste money on an ineffective workflow, so you invest in new hardware or machines that can handle the challenge. Or maybe you simply stagnate and stifle your growth by thinking too small, and the only way to escape this is through expansion: new offices, more staff, better location, a few new investors.

Now, you may associate expansion with moving to a new location, building new offices, creating new divisions within your team, or investing in large machines, and although I appreciate such images are bound to pop into your mind, I ask you to resist such affiliations. To expand is to spread your wings, which can come in many forms. Each mistake is different, remember, and each failure and faux pas leads you down a new and rocky road. So although expansion can result in new offices and machines, this isn't always the case, and to illustrate this point I'd like to reintroduce an inspiring someone from the opening pages of this book; Jordan Harbinger.

To recap Jordan's mistake, he hired friends and kept people within his business, The Art of Charm, for the wrong reasons.

You may even recall his shower-induced epiphany when he realised he searched for reasons to keep a rather worthless employee, and in an instant knew he'd taken a wrong turn somewhere along the way. Mistake in hand, Jordan set out to transform his failure into success, and it led him to expand the business, but not through fancy new offices or expensive machinery, but instead by partnering with somebody new.

'These days I don't mange them,' Jordan said after I asked him how he manages those friends who remain under the Art of Charm umbrella. 'I now have a business partner who's amazing at strategy and development, so he does all the hiring. Sure, I might throw my two cents in from time to time, and I help during the recruiting stage, but he does all the hiring and firing. This is great, not just because I don't have to deal with those situations anymore, but because my competencies lie elsewhere. I'm able to focus on other aspects of the business and ensure we continue to grow the right way.'

Within a few minutes of listening to Jordan, I realised he's the type of fun-loving individual who likes to meet new people, and as such, I imagine it would be nigh on impossible for him not to hire friends and those he knows. So, he had to find a different solution; a solution that allowed him to distance himself from the issue and make sure it didn't keep reoccurring.

'Anything you can do to compartmentalise it, the better,' he continued, telling me more about how he approaches things today. 'Sometimes I can't help but hire friends, because I meet someone and we start to hang out, and then I mention we're about to hire a new marketer. And they say, "Oh, I'm a great marketer who's made millions of dollars for my current company, but I'm looking for a new challenge." So, we interview them because this is the type of person we wish to have at The Art of Charm. But the thing is, they don't work directly for me, so I'm not the one who has to manage them and have those awkward situations.' You may say that this is a rather cowardly approach, but as Jordan said himself, 'People who say that have never had to fire a friend before.'

Now, the point here isn't about hiring friends or Jordan's initial mistake per se, it's about the decision he took to expand The Art of Charm with a new partner; a partner who took the mistake off his shoulders; a partner that allowed Jordan to focus on growing the business and doing what he does best. Was this a big decision to make? Absolutely! Did this cost money and require a big investment? Yes! Hiring a high level executive is huge, as is handing over that amount of control and responsibility. But in order to overcome the mistake and transform it into success (let alone ensure it doesn't happen again), Jordan and the team had to expand: the business, their operations, and the way they approached their day to day.

Sometimes you do need to expand your operations and business in order to grow and transform your mistake into a success. Sometimes it isn't about focusing on a niche, or even delving into new markets or ideas, but is about doubling up on what you do and taking it to the next level. If this means hiring a new executive, so be it. If this requires new staff and the type of resources that are sure to stretch your finances and sanity, fine. If this results in a new office, machine, or piece of software, then you do what you need to do. This is about you and yours, and your situation differs to mine, or Jordan's, or those of the other 162 people who feature in this book.

The point isn't to copy Jordan's fix, but to appreciate that you may have to expand what you're currently doing in order to transform your own mistakes into success. But what if you cannot expand or diversify, and what if focusing won't fix the issue at hand? Is there another option? There is, and on the surface it may seem like giving up, but I assure you it isn't, because the only time you truly give up is when you wave the white flag on your dream to change this world for the better.

INSPIRED BY STORIES FROM: JORDAN HARBINGER, DUANE JACKSON, FRASER DOHERTY, MIKE MCDERMOTT, MIKE EILERTSEN, BEN KRUEGER

START AGAIN

When you set out to start a new business and build a life on your own terms, the last thing you want to consider is the fact it may one day fail. And when I say fail, I don't mean the type of failure you can rekindle and turn around, I mean the end, that's it, closing the doors one final time. That's not to say it's the end of you, but sometimes a business or venture ends. In fact, the majority do, I'm afraid.

I suspect that barely a day goes by that you don't walk down the street and notice a shop or a restaurant having closed its doors. It happens, and although you don't wish to consider such a travesty, it's important that you're aware of it. But remember, the end of your business doesn't mean it's the end of you or your journey, and to finish up Stage Six: Reconstruction, we peek into the horrible world of having to start again. Of course, as you've already seen, starting again isn't always the worst thing in the world. Steve Olsher had to start again twice — after the dotcom bubble burst and the real-estate crash — yet these failures led to his life today; one full of freedom, purpose, and meaning. Dan Miller lost it all, owing large sums of money to the IRS. He had to start again from scratch, but this led him to the online world, and one full of opportunity. And Jayson Gaignard had to lose it all and let go of his empire, in order to build something far grander and long-lasting. I'm not here to say starting again is easy, or that it won't cripple you if it happens. You do not start a business to watch it fall, and reading a few words from a guy like me isn't going to take away the pain. But sometimes your mistakes and your failures lead to this regardless, although it does not mean it's the end for you.

Quite to the contrary, in fact, and one guy who rose from such despair goes by the name Richard; a man whose journey twisted and turned before it began to make any sense at all. Founder of Magic Rock Brewing, Richard Burhouse leads an up-and-coming brewery that not only produces tasty beer, *which I can attest to*, but has a brand that's among the finest I've seen.

When I sat down with Richard outside Leeds Town Hall one summer afternoon, I suspected he might share a tale about Magic Rock and how he and the team overcame one of the many issues a young brewing company tends to face. Instead, he transported me back to a few years before, reliving the story of his failed business that, had it not failed, would mean Magic Rock Brewing wouldn't exist at all.

'My previous business was built around a subscription model that sent craft beer directly to the customer's door each month,' Richard said, telling me all about how that business and Magic Rock have rather a lot in common.

You see, this failed venture came at a time when such a business model wasn't as popular. It was a period before Dollar Shave Club and the like, and Richard and his team could never quite build enough traction.

'The product was good,' he said, 'and our customers loved what we offered. But we could never make it viable because the demand wasn't quite high enough, whilst the costs were. It's expensive to source new beer each month, and to then post them directly to the customer. It was frustrating because we had a model that worked, and a product people liked, but we could never get it to the level we needed.'

Richard's mistakes ultimately came down to a lack of industry knowledge, I suppose. It's an idea that certainly had potential, but would always be difficult to scale. Of course, a few years after this, such models and businesses did begin to gain traction, so who knows what Richard could have created had he not shut his doors when he did.

Was he a man before his time? Possibly, but fear not because Richard found himself learning a great deal about the brewing industry during this period, and more importantly, developed a rich network of people. He already had a passion for beer and everything that came with it, and the failure of this business offered him the knowledge he needed to start a new one; and dare I say his true passion of opening his own brewery.

'I've always loved beer and taken an interest in brewing, hence why I started the first business. But my dream has always been to brew my own, and I'm not sure I'd have ever done this without everything I took from that first failed business.'

As he told me a few more tales about his past, and where it led him to today, I couldn't help but think how Richard's initial mistake and failure turned out to be the best thing that ever happened to him. Between his smile and the way his face lit up whilst discussing Magic Rock, it was clear that this was where his passion and true calling lies; not in a business that delivers beer to you each month, but rather one that creates it in the first place.

Remember, Magic Rock only began because one business failed, and although a failed brand should not be taken lightly — after all, any business closing its doors is a tough pill to swallow, because it leads to a lot of lost money, time, sleepless nights, and dreams — it's important to highlight the fact that starting again isn't necessarily the end of you or your world.

This isn't failure, nor is it the end; it's the harsh reality that not all businesses succeed. I think it's important that you appreciate this, but also that you don't place too much of your own personal success and worth within the walls of a single entity you create. Your journey reaches further than this, and although none of this is to say it makes starting again easy, it does help ensure you don't completely give up if the moment arrives. Because I'm afraid to say, sometimes focusing, diversifying, and expanding isn't enough, and every now and again you'll simply reach the end of that road. But not the end of your road, which I like to think is a good way to end Stage Six: Reconstruction, and begin our ascent to the next stage, Acceptance.

If it's during Stage Five: The Tipping Point when you open your eyes, then it's during Stage Six that you figure out which action to take. For some, this involves a small step and a tiny correction of course, whereas for others it's a much more fundamental shift. Whichever camp you may fit into, appreciate that it's this period when you truly turn things around and turn a bad time into a good one. It's during this stage that you take everything you've learned and implement it for the better. And whether this process takes days, weeks, months, or years, it's what you do during Stage Six that transforms where you are to where you'll soon be, and it's all of this that makes Stage Seven all the more delicious.

Acceptance is rather grand indeed, as it isn't only where you let go of your mistakes and failures and all those other hardships, but when you begin to appreciate a new meaning of success, freedom and happiness.

But, before we get to accepting all of this, let's quickly recap what you've just learned whilst reconstructing your world.

INSPIRED BY STORIES FROM: RICHARD BURHOUSE, DAN MILLER, GREG HICKMAN, STEVE OLSHER, DANNY INY, ALBERT GREISMYER, BRENTON HAYDEN, JOHN CORCORAN, KATE MATS, TOME MORKES, STEWART ROSS, TRENT DRYSMID, CLAY HEBERT

STAGE 6: TASKS & TAKEAWAYS

The following recaps what you've just read, sums up the main learnings, and provides a few actionable tasks you can implement into your world today. You can also download a free version of this workbook at: successfulmistake.com/takeaways

TOP TEN TAKEAWAYS FROM STAGE 6

1) It's during this stage of **reconstruction** that you right a few wrongs, and take your one time mistake by the scruff of the neck and show it who's boss.

2) Often, the best way to achieve this is to **focus** on what you're already doing, and dive further into the process so you perfect what you offer and who you offer this to.

3) Such **focus** can revolve around further niching into your industry, getting to know your customers better, involving them more in the process, and as often the case may be, taking your business/product/idea from the amateur leagues to the pros.

4) Of course, focusing on what you already do isn't always the answer, and this could lead you to **diversify**, which may include introducing new products, entering new markets, or doing what you're doing already but in a completely new way.

5) **Diversification** doesn't always come about because your initial offer or idea isn't good, but in order to make

sure what you do is sustainable and scaleable, you simply need to offer more, and in a more diverse fashion.

6) Sometimes what you're doing is the right thing to do, and the aspect that's holding you back is that you're not growing fast enough. During times like these, you may need to **expand** on your business, operations, and everything else.

7) Although **expansion** can include new offices and grander machinery, it often revolves around people and the team you're building, as this not only allows your business to grow, but let's you focus on what you do best.

8) As a final resort, you may sometimes have to **start again** and allow your old business/product/idea slip to the wayside.

9) Granted, **starting again** isn't an ideal situation (and is one you most likely don't wish to consider), but it often allows a far better idea and business to form in its place.

10) It's during *Stage Six: Reconstruction* that you take action and literally begin transforming your mistake into success. Where the previous stage focused on opening your eyes, it's here where you do, act and implement!

~ *()* ~

TOP TASKS FROM STAGE 6

1) Choose one project or idea that's taken place in the last year, and that has either failed or simply didn't live up to your expectations.

2) Based on this project, create two columns: What Went Right and What Went Wrong — and spend at least fifteen minutes adding as much as you can under both headings.

3) Then, based on these two lists, and everything else you know about this project, imagine you're given the opportunity to launch it all over again; only this time, you get to implement everything you've learned since. Considering focus, diversification, expansion, or starting again, decide which path would best apply, and write a short overview of why you believe this.

4) Finally, come up with five ideas you could implement that would result in a more successful project, and ideally, would lead to greater success in other parts of your business.

On their own, these tasks may seem strange, but as you work through this book you'll begin to appreciate how these actionable sections help you implement what you learn straight away.

Because remember, this book isn't here to simply inspire and entertain you, but also <u>educate</u> you at the same time.

And to make your life easier, you can download an interactive version of these Tasks & Takeaways, which lets you make notes within the PDF itself (and print it off), as well as watch a video tutorial where I go through each task one by one, and explain how and why they are relevant to you in the here-and-now.

Download your worksheet at: <u>successfulmistake.com/takeaways</u>

STAGE 7: TODAY'S TORTURE IS TOMORROW'S HAPPINESS

Have you seen the movie *500 Days of Summer*? It's the one with Zoey Deschanel and Gordon Joseph Levitt, that follows the lead character, Tom (Levitt), who falls in love with Summer *(Deschanel)* before she breaks his heart and leaves him in turmoil. It's a typical love story affair, and one with a real-world ending — in other words, they don't live happily ever after with a nice bow tied around it. After all, this is life we're talking about, and it rarely deals in bows and sprinkles.

Love, business, life in general… They don't always go according to plan.

In the movie, Tom works his way through the turmoil (shock, pain, bargaining, depression), until he reaches a tipping point and starts to reconstruct his life (which involves getting a new job and actually leaving the house), before finally, at the end of the movie, you see the look in his eyes as his moment of acceptance hits.

It's a wonderful moment when you're able to look back on your situation and smile.

It's the first morning you wake up after a loss and don't feel utterly drained and lifeless. It's the day you smile and it doesn't seem fake or forced. It's the time you believe in yourself and actually believe it. It's the moment you know you've turned the corner, because you accept where you are and what has happened, and this acceptance allows you to move on.

We all go through hardships in this world, and they're not always related to your business or work.

A life without times of such hardship doesn't exist, so it isn't about living a fulfilling life avoiding them or in spite of them, it's about pushing through them and figuring out a glorious lifestyle *because* of them. And although some might argue it's time that heals all wounds, I don't believe this to be true, because I think it's acceptance that guides you, and during Stage Seven: Acceptance, you complete your #greatmistake journey by figuring out what this is.

Nobody is saying that your life will be easy after this point, or free of mistakes and failure, but it's acceptance that shines a new light on who you are and what you're doing, and indeed where you've come from and where you're going.

In stages five and six, you opened your eyes and took action; begun the process of turning a bad time into a good one. From here, you can truly learn to not only ensure you don't make the same mistakes over and over again, but begin to develop the same sort of mindset as those you admire, and the type of approach to work and life that sets those at the top of their game apart from everyone else.

But more on this soon, because first you must focus on **hindsight**, **a new outlook**, and your **personal growth**, and the roles these play during this stage of **acceptance**.

I'll always recall what Michael O'Neal (founder and host of *The Solopreneur Hour*) said to me when he focused on the mistakes he made and the pain he felt all those years before starting his own business, because I feel it sums up this process of acceptance rather well; 'You only know what you know at the time.'

In other words, it's difficult to appreciate your mistakes and failures at the time, and it's hard to see past the pain and turmoil when you're struggling through it in the here and now.

No matter who you are and how much money you may have, I suspect this never changes, because you only ever know what you know. But it's here during Stage Seven: Acceptance that you look back and see your situation for what it was. You appreciate the lessons and the good that rose out of the bad, and you understand how that once upon a time pain has since developed into new ideas, motivation, and dedication. It's hard to see this when you're living through it, but during this stage of acceptance the pieces click into place; that's if you decide to complete the process and accept your mistakes and failures, and you choose to look back on this period and make a conscious effort to learn from it and let go of it. Because if all you do at this stage is sweep it under the carpet, continue to beat yourself up, pretend it wasn't as bad in the first place, or that it won't happen again then you may have come all this way for nothing.

Acceptance is exactly that; accepting what's been and what is and moving on with your head held high with the aim to make things better. So, before you read the rest of Stage Seven: Acceptance, take a deep breath and commit to a positive outlook, because when it comes to subjects like hindsight, you can both smile and grimace. Let's face it, hindsight's an annoying little parasite that laughs in your face as it says, 'Well, if only you knew this sooner, you wouldn't have had to suffer through all that pain and suffering.' I feel the frustration of hindsight too, and often consider what it would be like if I knew what I knew today when I first set out on this journey. But like Michael says, 'You only know what you know at the time.'

Instead think of hindsight as a somewhat annoying friend who says 'I told you so', but whose heart is in the right place. It isn't laughing at you, merely pointing out where you've come from so you ensure you move forward for the better. If you get to stage seven and don't approach things with this sort of mindset, you run the risk of making the same mistakes again and again, and although you may work through them and transform failure into success, wouldn't it be better to grow from this to the point where you don't make as many mistakes in the first place? This is what *Stage Seven* focuses on, and this is how we end your #greatmistake adventure.

You're nearly at the finish line, but let's first tackle that annoying yet wise friend of ours, hindsight…

THE WONDERFUL WORLD OF HINDSIGHT

When it comes to hindsight, it's easy to fall into both the 'glass half full' and 'glass half empty' categories, because on the one hand, if you always knew what you know today, you'd be a billionaire and an overall genius. It is indeed annoying, but it's also hindsight that allows you to learn and mature in the first place, and without it I dare say you'd make the same mistakes ad infinitum.

I believe that I am at the mercy of hindsight more than most, largely because of my overactive imagination and obsession towards the concept of 'what if'; in fact, my first novel, *Beyond Parallel*, centred around this entire notion of what could be, and it's something that haunts me to this day; what if I'd chosen this, done that, took this path instead of the other. Of course, researching and writing this book has helped me a great deal, because I've met dozens of inspiring people who have helped me figure things out through their own experiences.

The very nature of this book has been to ask them to look back on tough periods in their lives; times full of shame, disappointment, and frustration, to share the lessons they learned and show how all that pain developed into happiness. Each interview relied on hindsight to shine through and lead the way, because without it they would still only know what they knew back then. With it came growth and acceptance, and the ability to smile and laugh at a potentially devastating aspect of their past lives.

I'll be honest with you. In the past I've always had a 'glass half empty' outlook on hindsight, frustrated at its mocking and belittling ways. I'm happy to say that this is no longer the case, and if you take a single something from this book, I hope that it's a newfound appreciation for hindsight; it may well be that annoying friend who says 'I told you so', but it's also the friend that helps you transform failure into success, and stand shoulder to shoulder with those you admire. After all, this is the approach the world's most successful take, although it may not have always been the case. Take Craig Wolfe, for instance, the founder and CEO of CelebriDucks.

CelebriDucks is a rubber duck company with a difference; Craig and his team design and manufacture unique ducks that resemble the likes of Elvis Presley, Yoda, and James Dean. It's a marvellous company that leads their industry, and that continues to push the boundaries and set high standards to this day. But this success hasn't come without hardship, and Craig and co. almost lost it all when he became somewhat obsessed with a single, seemingly simple idea.

'Simply put, it was our greatest failure and success at the same time,' he said, describing the period that he decided to bring the manufacturing process back to America. 'We were already the only company who did all our designs and sculpting in the States, but we outsourced our manufacturing overseas. I wanted to bring the process back to America for a long time and revitalise the industry. It felt like the right thing to do, and I knew it would lead to new jobs and put our story and values on the map.'

It didn't take long for Craig to realise the undertaking of this idea, finding it difficult to source factories that could live up to his expectations. After all, CelebriDucks had become market leaders owing to their attention to quality and detail, so they couldn't accept anything less from their partners. After an exhausted search, Craig found an Ohio factory who believed they could fulfil everything they needed to, but despite their efforts and dedication, nothing seemed to work.

'It was bad,' Craig said. 'We ploughed through tens of thousands of dollars, but the factory just couldn't get the ducks to float or work. It was a huge problem because we had deadlines to meet, including big clients like Harley Davidson. We couldn't fail, but for the first time ever, I worried that we'd be unable to finish what we'd started.'

Craig and his team decided to take this risk for all the right reasons; not for money or market share, but in order to bring a lost industry and skill back to a country that brought it to life in the first place. You could argue his mistake came down to naivety or not researching things enough before taking action, but for the most part it was several elements that came together to cause this rather stressful upheaval. Thankfully, they hustled and bustled their way to the finish line, fulfilling their first big order at the last minute, although at this stage they still didn't have a solution. But then came their knights in shining armour...

'Finally, we found a factory in New York where the original rubber ducks were made. They could do everything we needed them to do, plus they had the expertise to do so. It was a huge relief, but we still had to move all our operations from the Ohio factory to the New York one — as you can imagine, this was an expensive mistake in its own right; but in the end, what nearly killed us created us. Our USA-made ducks are now our most popular product, and the fact that we design, sculpt, and make them all in America sets us apart. It's put our story on the map and has turned into our greatest asset, even though it began out of a huge mistake and failure.'

Listening to Craig talk about this period, which I can only imagine led to a lot sleepless nights and stress, I couldn't detect a hint of regret or remorse for what could have been. He spoke with such excitement and vigour, despite the fact that it had cost him money, pain, and so much more. Remember, CelebriDucks was already the world's leader in this type of product, so taking such a risk wasn't necessary. Craig could have quit. He could have looked back on things and done the number crunching, regretting the decisions he'd made. For a while, maybe he did, but he soon began to realise how beneficial this hardship was, and that without it they wouldn't have their story that sets them apart from their competitors.

With a 'glass half empty' outlook on this period, I'm sure his hindsight would look rather different, but because he embraces it, he's able to appreciate the good that grew out of it, and therefore accept the mistakes he made and see the failures they suffered through for what they were: a stepping stone and single step on their much grander journey.

Now, could he have appreciated this hindsight during the shock, pain, or bargaining? It's doubtful. Did this period shake him to the core and almost break him? I imagine so. Was he able to see all of this as he worked through his tipping point and reconstruction? Probably not, because he was too busy finding solutions and turning bad into good. But here, in Stage Seven: Acceptance, this is the stage when you're able to look back on where you've been, and you can focus on this glorious hindsight with a positive outlook or a negative one. How you choose to look at it is up to you, but I would encourage you to take a page out of Craig's book, because those successful individuals you look up to and admire tend to take the same positive outlook, too. Remember, this period must have drained Craig's life and caused a great deal of pain, and you'd maybe forgive him for giving up, or at the very least, feeling somewhat hard done by. After all, he took this risk with good intentions in mind, so he didn't deserve so much hardship. Instead he says things like, 'in the end, what nearly killed us created us.'

The truth is, *hindsight is* that annoying 'told you so' friend. It points out the obvious at the worst time. It offers you help when you no longer need it, much like banks are happy to offer you a loan when you have a bunch of cash already, but when you actually need it, they don't answer your calls. But it's also what gives you the ability to learn from your mistakes, and it's this knowledge that provides you with the power to *accept* where you've come from and let go of it. From here, you can develop a new outlook on life and work, meaning you don't only turn a single failure into success, but create lots of new successes on the back of it. This is where we turn our attention now, because it's here when your bright tomorrow begins.

INSPIRED BY STORIES FROM: CRAIG WOLFE, ARNOLD DU TOIT, CLAIRE MORELY JONES, CORBETT BARR, DEBBIE MILLMAN, MICHAEL O'NEAL, LAURA BENSON, SCOTT OLDFORD, TIM GRAHL, BRIAN FOLEY, JAMES EDER, JOSH SPRAGUE, LISA RAYNES, LINDA COLES, SHEEVAUN MORAN

A NEW WAY OF WORK & LIFE

You learn a lot about yourself, your business, industry, and audience during times of hardship and failure, but as I keep saying, this is both hard to see and to appreciate at the time. It isn't until you look back on this period with hindsight that the true picture presents itself, and it isn't until you accept where you are and where you've come from that you move forward. And although not every single mistake and failure will change your life and redefine how you live it, some of them will.

These tough periods can affect your wellbeing and workflow, and how you tackle your daily routine. They can force you to see your business in a totally new light.

I don't know about you, but when I consider how today's mistakes can fundamentally change everything about tomorrow (what I do, how I approach it, the purpose I share), I shiver and break out in a sweat because there are so many unknowns, and it is, quite frankly, terrifying. But it's also exciting because this new outlook on your business and life isn't based upon some off-the-cuff idea, it's based on genuine growth; and isn't growth what you strive towards each day? You want to grow as a person, and to grow your businesses, and dedicate everything you do to growing your world and those around you. In the next section we focus on **personal growth**, but before we get to that I'd like you focus on something more fundamentally business-like. The simple fact is, that when you look back on your mistakes and accept them, you'll undeniably alter your outlook and approach, and everything that comes with it; your business's structure, product, workflow, and so much more. In doing so, I can think of nobody better to focus on than the same man who opened this book; AJ Leon. A true inspiration throughout my own journey, and a massive influence on these very pages, AJ lives the life that many of us dream about, but too few ever dare to try.

If you choose to delve into Misfit Inc's work and projects, you'll discover a varied array of offerings ranging from humanitarian windmill building in Kenya to Tweetable gifts that bring you closer to your community. But the thing is, Misfit Inc didn't begin this way, and it's this that AJ considers to be his biggest mistake.

'When we first setup Misfit Inc, one of our largest mistakes was focusing solely on client work,' he said, whilst sitting in a Fargo hotel room, a few months before his first ever Misfit Conference. 'After all, it's the easy route to take. It's the low-hanging fruit. You can always figure out ways to find more clients and keep the ball rolling.'

I'd been following AJ for some time at this point, and had no idea that Misfit Inc offered services such as web design. I didn't know about their client work, but as he continued to share his tale it soon become obvious why.

'These days, our focus has flipped upside down,' he continued. 'We used to spend eighty percent of our time on client work and twenty percent on our own projects, but today we dedicate eighty percent of our resources to our own projects. We did this very deliberately, but it took some time. It's hard to claw away from something you rely on, and client work brings in cash, whereas your own projects are so risky and unknown.'

AJ's mistake ultimately came down to fear, and lack of belief that he'd be good enough and worthy enough to share his own projects with the world. It's an understandable one, and when you first begin a business — *any business* — ensuring you have money coming into your bank account remains a primary focus at all times. But it isn't so much AJ's mistake that blew me away, it's how this changed his entire approach to work and life.

'The main caveat I've taken from this experience is to live deliberately; to dig in my heels and clench my fists, and make sure I'm the one who decides what it is I do. This might seem simple, and you may think you do this already, but I assure you most people don't.'

As you may recall from earlier, AJ went through this issue

previously in his life, whilst sitting in his Manhattan corner office with a hefty wage in hand. He knew that if he didn't change his path, he'd never escape his corporate imprisonment, and likewise, if he continued to focus most of his resources on client work, he'd remain in a similar prison of his own making.

Living through these mistakes forced AJ to appreciate a new outlook on life, and it didn't only alter Misfit Inc as a business, but changed his own personal approach to each day, too; to live deliberately.

'I now live a life of my own choosing,' he said, smiling proudly. 'My time since leaving the comfort of my finance job has been a constant and iterative journey that takes me further and further away from the shore each day. As entrepreneurs and artists, it's a constant battle we face: one where we have to choose between doing something that matters and challenging ourselves, or choosing to take the safe and comfortable option. Our gut reaction is to stay safe, whether that involves keeping your job or a client or whatever. But our job as artists and creators is to stiff arm this mentality and continue to sail away from the shore; to not allow safety and security to govern our work and how we choose to spend each day.'

The thing is, despite his inspiring ways, AJ didn't figure this out straight away. He made mistakes whilst working in the corporate world, and brought these same mistakes into Misfit Inc's early days. Like Michael O'Neal said, 'You only now what you know at the time.' So, although AJ lives a deliberate, passionate, and meaningful life today, he didn't always have it figured out. He made mistakes and he suffered and stumbled, but it was also this suffering and longing that helped him to appreciate a new outlook on not only his business, but on his life as a whole.

And if you're anything like me, the very idea of this both excites and terrifies you! This life you're leading right now — whether you have enough money or not, or whether you consider yourself happy or not — is comfortable and safe, and although you may like the idea of changing and inviting a new way of life into your world, actually committing to it is another thing all together. But this is what successful people do, and it's the very reason this book exists in the first place. It's here to help guide you through your mistake and failures, and not only survive them, but thrive *because* of them. It's the sort of acceptance that completes your journey, and it's this type of growth that helps you become the person you want to become; helps your business, products, and everything that comes with it become the best they can be.

Although this is both exciting and terrifying, you're not alone in feeling like this; everyone who features in this book has felt the same way. We are, after all, part of the same human race, and we all tend to feel each and every day.

So, if you work your way through these seven stages, and then inglorious hindsight shows its somewhat annoying face, making you look at things in a different way, and giving you a new outlook on your business and life, it's okay. It's okay to be afraid. It's okay to doubt. It's okay if your first reaction is to ignore it or pretend it isn't real. It's okay to feel, because you're a real human person, after all.

We started this book discussing how mistakes and failure invite change into your life, and as a species we're not very good with change. The very notion of a new outlook invites change, too, but this change isn't based on a whim or momentary lapse, but on genuine growth. In fact, it isn't change at all, it's evolution, it's progression.

Such growth is powerful indeed, and although it may terrify you, it tends to lead you down a good path, so be sure to not only accept where you've come from (your mistakes and failures) and where you are (what you've reconstructed out of this), but also accept where you're going, too. After all, if this journey you're on isn't about growth — you and your business growing — what is it about?

This brings us to the next section, **personal growth**, because although a new outlook like this is both potentially game-changing for you and your business, I honestly believe that it's *you* that remains the most important piece of the puzzle at all times.

Great businesses aren't built on great products or great ideas, they feed on the process of great people becoming ever-greater people. I've personally learned a lot on this book-writing journey, but this may be my grandest lesson of all.

INSPIRED BY STORIES FROM: AJ LEON, BRENTON HAYDEN, CAPRICE BOURRET, CARLY WARD, CHRISTINE RICHMOND, JEN GRESHAM, JUDITH WRIGHT, MARY JUETTEN, PAM SLIM, TONY ABBOTT, ZEKE CAMUSIO, SHEEVAUN MORAN, ETHAN AUSTIN, HELEN TODD, LISA RAYNES, LUKE HODSON, TOM MORKES, TOM GREVESEN

PERSONAL GROWTH & YOU

I imagine that when you first picked up this book, you expected it to offer a lot of business-related ideas that would help you develop your business, and I hope it's lived up to these expectations. Nevertheless, I also hope you appreciate that these pages offer a great deal more than this, because although this book is designed to help you grow your business, it's also here to help you grow as a person.

As an entrepreneur, you are your business. As a creator and innovator and artist, what you achieve in life, and how successful you become, comes down to how much you grow as a person. Which is why we've left **personal growth** until the bitter end, because it needs to remain fresh in your mind.

Of course, we've touched upon health and wellbeing and personal evolution throughout this book, and we've done so because it's paramount. It's fundamental to the journey that you're on.

As much as I've loved listening to successful and inspirational people talk about how they overcame their mistakes and failures, and built powerful businesses on the back of them, the biggest pleasure I've taken from this process is seeing them smile as they realise how far they've come, and how they've progressed and matured as people.

Businesses become great because of the greatness of the people involved; indeed, these people become greater and greater as time wears on. As you become a better and more well-rounded individual, your business, your products and everything that revolves around this (staff, customers, community) benefits.

You are an entrepreneur. You are a self-made human being who's making it all happen on your own terms. You are the nuts and bolts. Never undermine how important your own personal growth is.

You can learn so much from the people who feature in this

book; every single one of them has valuable advice designed to help you grow your business, improve your bottom line, reach new people, and so on. But the grandest and simplest lesson they have to share with you is that they are who they are, and that they have all focused on themselves personally. Srinivas Rao, for instance, is a fine gentleman who embodies this idea of personal growth rather well.

You may remember Srini from earlier, the main man behind the Unmistakeable empire (including the podcast, books, and much more), and you may also recall how his big mistake surrounded external accolades and filling his portfolio with as many fancy names as possible.

'I think my biggest mistake was getting caught up in the ego-driven pursuit of a life that looks good on paper,' said Srini, to refresh your memory. 'I wanted the big names on my resume, and think I wanted the external accolades more than the work itself. Of course, this resulted in it all falling apart like a stack of cards.'

Like so many of us, Srini searched for meaning and purpose, and as most folk do, he turned to university and business school, picturing himself in a corner office as he nurtured a healthy salary each month. He chased what we're all supposed to chase. He wanted success, and there's a certain preconceived way to go about it. As you know, this is exactly what successful entrepreneurs do not do, but Srini had to suffer through a few mistakes before it clicked into place.

We won't revisit Srini's complete tale, because we focused on that during Stage One and Fear. The reason I share his story with you again right now is, it was during his mistake that he grew as a person and began to appreciate a new approach — not just for business, but for his life in general.

And he summed this up when he said, 'I find intrinsic value in everything I do now, which I didn't used to. It's a lot more fun, and the real creativity shines through once you focus on this.'

The moment that Srini talked about his purist view of intrinsic value, I realised why he's found the success he has, and why he continues to grow and build his community to this day. This acceptance didn't bring new product ideas or business plans, it brought a real sense of personal growth that ignited passion, bringing purpose and meaning into everything he does.

So, although Stage Seven: Acceptance has the power to potentially turn a once good business idea into a great one, the greatest benefit of all (indeed, during this entire journey) is the personal growth on offer. Good ideas, products, and services are not the determining factors behind a successful business, it's the people who drive them, manage them, and ensure they grow in the right direction. And because you're human and have all the faults and frailties that come with being human, you too may lose focus and push towards a bunch of external accolades that seem great on the surface, but offer so little to your actual worth. This is what Srini uncovered during his own great mistake, and he summed it up well when he said, 'Spending so much of my life in pursuit of things that brought no real meaning was my biggest failure.'

Not just any old failure, but his biggest of all.

These are the revelations Stage Seven can offer, but only if you're open to change and the fact that it may present you with a complete new way of living. It's a scary and daunting thought, but it's this that drives successful people to be successful in the first place. I don't mean in terms of having money, fame or power, I mean real success; happiness, freedom, passion, purpose, meaning and drive.

Folk like Srini had to go through a few personal hardships before they personally grew like this, but after reading this book it's my hope that you don't have to. And although we're now at the end of your #greatmistake journey, we're not quite finished, because as powerful as acceptance can be, should you choose to truly embrace it, it means little if you don't move onward with the right kind of mindset; the sort of approach Srini and everyone else in this book utilise on a daily basis.

But before we get to your special bonus stage, where we round up this adventure, let's recap the ins and outs of Stage Seven and place you in the right frame of mind.

INSPIRED BY STORIES FROM: SRINIVAS RAO, ARI MEISEL, BRIANA BORTEN, CHARLIE WILD, DEREK FLANZRAICH, EVO TERRA, MARS DORIAN, ISLA WOLSON, KRISTY OUSTALET, LUKE HODGSON, MICHAEL O'NEAL, MITCH JOEL, NAOMI TIMPERELY, NICOLE WELCH, PAUL KEMP, RACHEL ELNAUGH, DESIREE EAST, HRIS CERRONE, FRANCIS PEDRAZA, JENNY BLAKE

STAGE 7: TASKS & TAKEAWAYS

The following recaps what you've just read, sums up the main learnings, and provides a few actionable tasks you can implement into your world today. You can also download a free version of this workbook at: successfulmistake.com/takeaways

TOP TEN TAKEAWAYS FROM STAGE 7

1) It's during **acceptance** when you complete your process, but only if you let go of you mistakes and failures, and accept them for what they are; lessons.

2) It's often hard to do this without **hindsight**, although the very notion of hindsight can be both powerful and damaging.

3) With a negative outlook, **hindsight** keeps you locked into these seven stages because you refuse to let go and move forward, whereas a positive outlook allows you to learn, grow, evolve, and accept the journey you're on — and indeed the journey that lies ahead.

4) It's also during this stage that you may develop a **new outlook**, not just regarding your business and work, but how you live your life overall and the purpose that drives this.

5) Such a **new outlook** potentially creates a lot of change and unknowns, but this isn't change for change's sake, rather evolution based on progression, growth, and

everything you've learned up until this point.

6) Arguably the greatest benefit from acceptance isn't the new outlook on your business, rather the **personal growth** you go through yourself.

7) It's this **personal growth** that helps you define what success means to you, but again this only happens if you accept it and embrace it; even if it presents change and an outlook that differs to what you know and have always wanted.

8) Simply put, your business doesn't become great based on the products you create and the services you offer, rather the people who drive all of this, including you, and it's your own **personal growth** that determines so much.

9) Overall, **acceptance** is a fantastic stage of your journey, as it presents a great deal of hope and opportunity that offers you the chance to fulfil your potential.

10) But **acceptance** is also a worrying and often terrifying period, as it may create an outlook you're not used to. Such fear is fine, but it's important to remember that this is borne out of evolution and progression, and that it's this that leads you to bigger and better ideas.

~ () ~

TOP TASKS FROM STAGE 7

1) You've just read about an array of authority leaders sharing their greatest business mistake; it's now time for you to consider what your grandest mistake of all is, related to business in some form, so spend a few minutes thinking about this, reliving it, and allowing it to consume you.

2) Using hindsight, write a list of each positive lesson you've taken from this big mistake; no matter how big or small the lesson may be.

3) Based on this list of lessons, choose the three you consider to have had the largest impact on you — not just in your business, but within your personal life, too.

4) Finally, using your current project/business/idea that you're working on, consider whether you are currently using these three key lessons to good effect, and whether you are or are not, commit to implementing these lessons into your project/business /idea immediately.

On their own, these tasks may seem strange, but as you work through this book you'll begin to appreciate how these actionable sections help you implement what you learn straight away.

Because remember, this book isn't here to simply inspire and entertain you, but also to educate you at the same time.

And to make your life easier, you can download an interactive version of these Tasks & Takeaways, which lets you make notes within the PDF itself (and print it off), as well as watch a video tutorial where I go through each task one by one, and explain how and why they are relevant to you in the here and now.

Download your worksheet at: successfulmistake.com/takeaways

WELCOME TO YOUR SUCCESSFUL MISTAKE

And so our journey together comes to a close. You should be proud of yourself for working through these marvellous seven stages that not only help you transform a mistake into a success, but also help you to appreciate the grander value of what success actually means to you in the first place.

You've gone through these stages one by one, and although sometimes your mistakes may follow this path, there are occasions when they will not.

The order may get jumbled up, and you may not experience each stage every time you slip into shock or pain, because not all mistakes send you into a depression, for instance.

As such, this book doesn't provide a definitive blueprint of what your mistakes look like each and every time, but now that you understand and appreciate how these seven stages work, you will be able to adapt and overcome whatever stands in your way.

The truth is, no two mistakes are ever the same, even if they seem that way on the surface. You may turn one epic failure into a giant success, but that doesn't mean that next time will require exactly the same approach. But now you have the know-how to turn a bad time into a good one, just like those you admire, and just like those who feature among these very pages.

I imagine you chose to read this book to learn from some of the world's finest, and although these pages focus on an imperative aspect of the entrepreneurial journey that has the power to make or break you, transforming your mistakes into success is, to an extent, a means to an end. You may find this an odd way to end this narrative, but I assure you it isn't, because once you understand and appreciate how to overcome your failures like you now do, your journey simply begins to take shape. After all, you're a go-getting individual who has embarked on a life that most people only dream about, so it's safe to say you'll stumble a great deal when you take new risks, build new businesses, and attempt to change the world for the better.

It's important that you know how to overcome such hardship, mistakes, and failures, but surely your grander aim is to avoid as many of these as you can in the first place. This takes us all the way back to the beginning of this book, and a rather simple sentiment of Mark Schaefer's... 'Here's the secret to business success: Don't make big mistakes.'

You're a self-starter who pushes the boundaries, so you'll continue to make mistakes and fail, and some of them will be larger than others, dragging rather large consequences in their wake. But you can avoid many of them, especially the big ones.

One of the biggest differences between successful people and those who haven't quite made it, is that truly successful individuals spot these issues before they have chance to build, and nip them in the bud before they grow into something painful. It doesn't make them immune to failure, but it gives them far better odds of success. And although we've tackled several warning signs during Stage One of this book, they only take you so far if you don't possess a particular type of mindset, outlook, and approach.

That is why we've finished this book focusing on you and your personal growth, and the notion that you need the bravery to accept that the path ahead may differ to the one that you've been leading; possibly the one that you've spent years dreaming about.

Such change is tough for anyone, and offers a terrifying concoction of unknowns with the power to cripple even the most confident of people.

Nevertheless, if I've learned a single lesson after interviewing 163 people who possess this type of successful mindset, it's that they embrace change, and move into acceptance with a positive outlook, and learn from everything they've done and everywhere they've been; *mistakes, failures and all*). They not only understand how to tackle these seven stages, but how to avoid them in the first place, and how to sprint through them if they happen to arise.

I don't intend to detract from this book in any way, nor underplay the importance of everything you've uncovered on this journey, but it's important that you appreciate that this book doesn't provide all the answers, and that it merely marks the beginning of so much more.

Understanding and appreciating your mistakes and failures — what they look like and how they form, the process you go through, and how to work through each stage, the many lessons to take from each, even during those somewhat hopeless and worthless periods, the growth, possibility, opportunity, and the ability to turn a decent idea into a life-changing one and indeed the growth you take from all of this, both for your business and your personal self — offers the potential to redefine the journey you're on and the business you're building, but my hope is that you'll desire more, because building a business is one thing, but crafting a legacy is another, and it's this that differentiates so many successful people from the rest of the pack.

So what now?

Well, this bookmarks the beginning of your journey, and the process of understanding and appreciating these seven stages offers you the means to take a few giant steps. You can't buy such a successful mindset or simply click your fingers; you earn it, and you earn it by thinking differently to the vast majority.

The workbooks, tasks, and takeaways that accompany these pages help you do this, as does everything else that takes place in *The Successful Mistake* universe — of which, as far as I'm concerned, you're now a valuable member. But as helpful and valuable as content, knowledge, exercises, and stories can be, everything comes back to you. Do you want a business or a legacy? Would you like to make money or make a real difference? Do you want read about those who feature in this book or be the type of person who appears in it?

The choice and everything that comes with it is yours, and I hope after working through these seven stages, you've not only been entertained and educated, but inspired to approach your business and life in a new light. I certainly have, and I can honestly say writing this book has changed how I live and approach my day.

But this isn't about me; it's about you.

It's about you taking everything you've just read, all those stories you've just devoured, and learning from them so you don't suffer the same pain as those that you admire have. Beyond this, it's about you figuring out what success means to you, and fulfilling your potential as soon as you can. You're a busy visionary with dreams to tackle and no time to waste, so go forth and create your own version of a successful mistake.

THANKS FOR READING

You've made it to the end of your #greatmistake, and the time has come for you to move onward and upward. It's been an absolute pleasure involving you in this adventure, and I'd like to say a big thank you for choosing this book over the hordes of others that exist in the world. I value you, and I only hope you've taken a lot of value from these pages, too.

Of course, this isn't the end of your journey, nor your time with me. In many ways, we've simply scratched the surface, because it's now time for you to figure out what success means to you and dedicate your life to it. Because in itself, overcoming mistakes, failure, and adversity isn't enough, for it's those who truly embrace what it means to be successful, happy, and free that make the biggest difference in this world.

You now have a choice to make, and it's to either settle for a business or build a meaningful legacy.

After reading *The Successful Mistake*, I hope it's the latter, and if this is the case then I have a great deal more to share with you. But let's leave that for another day, for right now you have a book to reflect on and a few next steps to take. Which begs the question: *what do you now that you've finished the book?*

STEP 1: VISIT SUCCESSFULMISTAKE.COM/EXTRAS

A special Extras Pack awaits you, designed to take everything you've read to the next level. This includes the complete set of interactive workbooks, an exclusive video course, and a few other surprises that await you. Grab your Extras Pack by visiting SuccessfulMistake.com/Extras >>

STEP 2: JOIN THE SUCCESSFUL MISTAKE COMMUNITY

Surround yourself with like-minded individuals who are ready to take things to the next level. This private community offers exclusive content and an experience designed to help you achieve success. Join for free by visiting tdog.co/fb-successful >>

STEP 3: LEAVE AN HONEST REVIEW ON AMAZON

You're a person with thoughts and opinions, so don't be shy. Not only do your honest reviews help me improve as a writer, but they introduce readers just like you to this very book. Write your short and honest review by visiting smarturl.it/successful >>

Thank you once again for joining me on this reading adventure. I only hope you've gathered a great deal of value from it. But again, your journey has only just begun, so delve deeper down the rabbit hole and follow those three simple steps.

Beyond this; don't by shy. I'm here to serve you and support you, so any time you have a question, please reach out to me at matt@turndog.co.

All that's left to do is to introduce you to a few friends of mine *(well, 163 of them, to be precise…)*

INTRODUCING THOSE WHO FEATURE IN THIS BOOK

AJ Leon

Misfit-inc.com

Alan Kipping-Ruane

TriGuyCoaching.com

Albert Griesmayr

AlbertGriesmayr.com

Alexander Franzen

AlexanderFranzen.com

Alexis Grant

Alexisgrant.com

Andrew Cooper

ApCooper.co.uk

Andrew Helm

RevolutionsBrewing.co.uk

Ari Meisel

Lessdoing.com

Arnold du Toit

Drive-Daddy.com

Ben Krueger

CashFlowPodcasting.com

Bernadette Jiwa

TheStoryofTelling.com

Brenton Hayden

RentersWarehouse.com

Brian Foley

BuddyTruk.com

Brian Gardner

Copyblogger.com

Brian Horn

Authorityalchemy.com

Briana Borten

Brianaborten.com

Caprice Bourret

Capricebourret.com

Carly Ward

YES-EducationUK.com

C.C. Chapman

CC-Chapman.com

Cesar Abeid

CesarAbeid.com

Charlie Kemp

Splitpixel.co.uk

Charlie Wild

YawnCreative.com

Chris Brogan

ChrisBrogan.com

Chris Cerrone

CerroneShow.com

Chris Sands

ChrisSands.co.uk

Christine Richmond

FreebirdAccountancy.co.uk

Claire Morley Jones

HR180.co.uk

Claud Williams

DreamNation.co.uk

Clay Hebert

ClayHebert.com

Colin Wright

ExcileLifestyle.com

Corbett Barr

Fizzle.co

Craig Wolfe

CelebriDucks.com

Dan Miller

48Days.com

Dana Humphrey

WhgitegatePR.com

Danny Fein

Litographs.com

Danny Iny

Mirasee.com

Dave Conrey

FreshRag.com

Dave Hirskchopp

DavesGourmet.com

Dave Kerpen

LikeableLocal.com

Dave Ursillo

DaveUrsillo.com

Dean Phillips

DeanPhillips.net

Debbie Millman

SterlingBrands.com

Derek Flanzraich

Greatist.com

Desiree East

DesireeEast.com

Dorie Clark

DorieClark.com

Duane Jackson

Supdate.com

Ellory Wells

ElloryWells.com

Emerson Spartz

EmersonSpartz.com

Emma Agese

AIG.com

Erin Blaskie

ErinBlaskie.com

Ethan Austin

GiveForward.com

Evo Terra

EvoTerra.com

Francis Pedraza

Invisible.Email

Fraser Doherty

Superjam.co.uk

Gary Butterfield

JuiceLimited.co.uk

Grant Baldwin

GrantBaldwin.com

Greg Hickman

Sytem.ly

Greg Smuk

Splitpixel.co.uk

Helen Todd

SocialitySquared.com

Isla Wilson

RubyStarAssociates.co.uk

Jacob Hill

TheLazyCamper.co.uk

Jaime Masters

EventualMillionaire.com

James Clear

JamesClear.com

James Eder

TheBeansGroup.com

James Smith

Asafe.com

Jared Easley

StarveTheDoubts.com

Jared O'Toole

Under30Experiences.com

Jason Gracia

SavvyHippos.com

Jayson Gaignard

MastermindTalks.com

Jeet Banerjee

JeetBanerjee.com

Jeff Bullas

JeffBullas.com

Jeff Goins

GoinsWriter.com

Jen Gresham

EverydayBright.com

Jenny Blake

JennyBlake.me

Jim Hopkinson

Mirasee.com

Jimmy Varley

OnlyProjects.co.uk

Joanna Davies

BlackWhiteDenim.com

Joanna Penn

TheCreativePenn.com

Jocy Hunter

JocelynHunter.co.uk

Joey Coleman

DesignSymphony.com

John Corcoran

SmartBusinessRevolution.com

John Lee Dumas

EoFire.com

John Wheelwright

JCJoel.com

Johnny B Truant

JohnnybTruant.com

Jon Crawford

JonCrawford.com

Jordan Harbinger

TheArtofCharm.com

Josh Sprague

OrangeMud.com

Judith Wright

WrightAngleMarketing.com

Kate Mats

KateMats.com

Kate Northrup

KateNorthrup.com

Kristi Hines

KristiHines.com

Kristin Thompson

SpeakServeGrow.com

Kristy Oustalet

KristyOustalet.com

Laura Benson

JeanneBeatrice.com

Liam Paterson

Dizinga.com

Linda Coles

BlueBanana.com

Lindsey F Rainwater

LindsetRainwater.com

Linsi Brownson

SparkCollaborative.com

Lisa Haggis

LisaHaggis.com

Lisa Raynes

RaynesArchitecture.co.uk

Luke Hodson

AwesomeMerchandise.com

Mauricio Geraud

Mgeraudm.Blogspot.com

Maggie Patterson

MaggiePatterson.com

Maneesh Sethi

Pavlok.com

Marianne Cantwell

Free-Range-Humans.com

Mark Manson

MarkManson.net

Mark Schaefer

BusinessGrow.com

Mark Seaman

RevolutionsBrewing.co.uk

Mars Dorian

MarsDorian.com

Marsha Shandur

YesYesMarsha.com

Mary Juetten

Traklight.com

Matt Cheuvront

ProofBranding.com

Mike Eilertsen

Mike-Eilertsen.co.za

Mike McDermott

Freshbooks.com

Michael O'Neal

Solopreneur.Hour.com

Mitch Joel

TwistImage.com

Moe Abdou

33Voices.com

Naomi Timperley

NaomiTimperley.co.uk

Natalie Sisson

SuitcaseEntrepreneur.com

Neil Patel

NeilPatel.com

Nick Simms

Accenture.com

Nick Unsworth

LifeonFire.com

Nicole Welch

RapWithNic.com

Nicole Baldinu

WebinarNinja.co

Ollie Lewis

LewisTrottDesign.com

Omar Zenhom

WebinarNinja.co

Paige Arnof-Fenn

MavensandMoguls.com

Pamela Slim

PamelaSlim.com

Paul Kemp

TheAppGuy.co

Peter Harrington

SimVenture.co.uk

Rachel Elnaugh

RachelElnaugh.com

Rameet Chawla

Fueled.com

Richard Burhouse

MagicRockBrewing.com

Ron Holt

TwoMaidsFranchise.com

Ross Kemp

ASAPWatercraft.com

Sam Tarantino

Groovesharks.org

Sati Salona

HomeInstead.co.uk

Scott Oldford

goInfinitus.com

Sean Platt

SterlingandStone.net

Sharon Herrman

ZeldasSong.com

Sheevaun Moran

SheevaunMoran.com

Sheila Viers

SheilaViers.com

Srinivas Rao

UnmistakeableCreative.com

Stephanie Roper

WardrobeAngel.co.uk

Steve Olsher

SteveOlsher.com

Stewart Ross

WharfedaleBrewery.com

Tabitha Naylor

TabithaNaylor.com

Tea Silvestre

StoryBistro.com

Temi Koleowo

BusinessFirstSteps.co.uk

Thomas Frank

CollegeInfoGeek.com

The Tielman Twins (Mike & Rick)

DoitwithMeraki.com

Tim Grahl

OutthinkGroup.com

Tom Ewer

LeavingWorkBehind.com

Tom Greveson

RevolutionViewing.co.uk

Tom Morkes

TomMorkes.com

Tony Abbott

Reactiv.co.uk

Trent Dyrsmid

BrightIdeas.co

Vernon Ross

VernonRoss.com

Will Trott

LewisTrottDesign.com

Zeke Camusio

DigitalAptitude.com

Zoe Jackson

LivingTheDreamCompany.co.uk

Thank You, All.

You Made This Book What It Is

ABOUT MATTHEW TURNER

Hi, my name is Matthew Turner, and I'm an author and storyteller who works with entrepreneurs, founders and creative thinkers to build thriving legacies that light a fire within them.

I've also decided to write this short bio in the first person, because I rather dislike third person bios. So, if you enjoy third person bios, I'm sorry for not being sorry.

Anyway, after interviewing 163 authority figures, I've unearthed how successful people overcome failure and adversity, not only ensuring they don't ruin their livelihood through their mistakes, but form their greatest ideas out of them.

The Successful Mistake marks the beginning of this journey, although the Successful universe continues to grow with programmes, courses, workshops, training sessions, mastermind communities, and much more to help go-getters and success-seekers fulfil their potential.

A true storyteller by nature, I've also written three novels including the acclaimed *I Unlove You*), a series of short stories, and I've even worked with the occasional client to ensure they take their storytelling to the next level.

This rather sums me up, although when I'm not writing, I live in the North of England with my son, George (or as I like to call him, Kid Turndog), and my partner in crime, Rosanna, where the three of us continue to fulfil our own version of success, freedom, and happiness.

You can learn more about me and my writing by visiting:

successfulmistake.com/extras